Union Public Library
1980 Morris Avenue
Union, N.J. 07083

P9-DZX-871

Volume equivalents

IMPERIAL	METRIC	IMPERIAL	METRIC
1fl oz	30ml	15fl oz	450ml
2fl oz	60ml	16fl oz	500ml
2$\frac{1}{2}$fl oz	75ml	1 pint	600ml
3$\frac{1}{2}$fl oz	100ml	1$\frac{1}{4}$ pints	750ml
4fl oz	120ml	1$\frac{1}{2}$ pints	900ml
5fl oz ($\frac{1}{4}$ pint)	150ml	1$\frac{3}{4}$ pints	1 liter
6fl oz	175ml	2 pints	1.2 liters
7fl oz ($\frac{1}{3}$ pint)	200ml	2$\frac{1}{2}$ pints	1.4 liters
8fl oz	240ml	2$\frac{3}{4}$ pints	1.5 liters
10fl oz ($\frac{1}{2}$ pint)	300ml	3 pints	1.7 liters
12fl oz	350ml	3$\frac{1}{2}$ pints	2 liters
14fl oz	400ml	5$\frac{1}{4}$ pints	3 liters

Weight equivalents

IMPERIAL	METRIC	IMPERIAL	METRIC
$\frac{1}{2}$oz	15g	5$\frac{1}{2}$oz	150g
$\frac{3}{4}$oz	20g	6oz	175g
scant 1oz	25g	7oz	200g
1oz	30g	8oz	225g
1$\frac{1}{2}$oz	45g	9oz	250g
1$\frac{3}{4}$oz	50g	10oz	300g
2oz	60g	1lb	450g
2$\frac{1}{2}$oz	75g	1lb 2oz	500g
3oz	85g	1$\frac{1}{2}$lb	675g
3$\frac{1}{2}$oz	100g	2lb	900g
4oz	115g	2$\frac{1}{4}$lb	1kg
4$\frac{1}{2}$oz	125g	3lb 3oz	1.5kg
5oz	140g	4lb	1.8kg

everyday
easy

Freeze-Ahead meals

Based on content previously published
in *The Illustrated Kitchen Bible*
and *The Illustrated Quick Cook*

everyday easy

Freeze-Ahead meals

casseroles • hearty soups
pizzas • one-pots • oven bakes

Union Public Library
1980 Morris Avenue
Union, N.J. 07083

LONDON, NEW YORK, MELBOURNE,
MUNICH, AND DELHI

US Editors Rachel Bozek, Liza Kaplan

Editor Shashwati Tia Sarkar

Project Art Editors Elly King, Kathryn Wilding

Senior Jackets Creative Nicola Powling

Managing Editor Dawn Henderson

Managing Art Editor Marianne Markham

Senior Production Editor Jennifer Murray

Production Controller Poppy Newdick

DK INDIA

Editorial Manager Glenda Fernandes

Designer Neha Ahuja

Editor Alicia Ingty

Assistant Designer Nidhi Mehra

Assistant Editor Megha Gupta

DTP Coordinator Sunil Sharma

DTP Operator Saurabh Challariya

Material first published in *The Illustrated Kitchen Bible,* 2008
and *The Illustrated Quick Cook,* 2009
This edition first published in the United States in 2010
by DK Publishing, 375 Hudson Street
New York, New York 10014

10 11 12 13   10 9 8 7 6 5 4 3 2 1
178707—October 2010

Copyright © 2008, 2009, 2010 Dorling Kindersley Limited
Text copyright © 2008, 2009, 2010 Dorling Kindersley Limited
All rights reserved

Without limiting the rights under copyright reserved above, no part
of this publication may be reproduced, stored in or introduced into
a retrieval system, or transmitted, in any form, or by any means
(electronic, mechanical, photocopying, recording, or otherwise),
without the prior written permission of both the copyright owner
and the above publisher of this book.
Published in Great Britain by Dorling Kindersley Limited.

A catalog record for this book is available
from the Library of Congress.

ISBN 978-0-7566-6732-0

DK books are available at special discounts when purchased in bulk
for sales promotions, premiums, fund-raising, or educational use.
For details, contact: DK Publishing Special Markets, 375 Hudson
Street, New York, New York 10014 or SpecialSales@dk.com.

Printed and bound in Singapore by Tien Wah Press

Discover more at
www.dk.com

CONTENTS

Batch and freeze

Double your cooking one night and freeze half for easy batch cooking, or freeze a full batch if you have time. Always cool completely before freezing, and thaw slowly—it is safer and will help retain the food's flavor and texture.

FOOD		PACKAGING	STORAGE	DEFROST
	SOUPS AND STOCKS Once cooked, let stand to cool completely, then pack into portions as needed. Don't freeze in oversized portions, as defrosting will take too long.	Pack in sealable plastic containers or freezer bags. The liquid will expand a little, so leave room for this. Stocks can be spooned into ice cube trays. Once frozen, remove from the tray and transfer to a freezer bag and seal.	Soups for up to 3 months. Stocks for up to 6 months.	Thaw overnight in the refrigerator, then reheat in a pan until piping hot, or heat in the microwave on high for a few minutes.
	SAUCES These take up little space in the freezer. If sauces call for the addition of egg yolk or cream, omit and add later. Cool completely before freezing.	Freeze in sealable freezerproof containers, bags, or ice cube trays. If using ice cube trays, once frozen, remove from the tray, transfer to a freezer bag, and seal. Leave air space for expansion.	Up to 3 months.	Thaw overnight in the refrigerator, then reheat in a pan until piping hot, or heat in the microwave on high for a few minutes.
	CASSEROLES AND CURRIES Fatty meats can go rancid after a while in the freezer, so choose lean cuts. When doubling up recipes, be careful not to over season; $1^1/_2$ times the usual is often enough.	Freeze in sealable freezer bags or foil containers, or ladle into rigid sealable plastic containers. Make sure meat is well covered by the liquid, otherwise it will dry out.	Up to 3 months.	Thaw overnight in the refrigerator, then reheat in a pan until piping hot, or heat in the microwave on high for a few minutes. Take extra care that the meat is really hot before serving and do not reheat more than once.
	PIES AND TARTS Baking is the ideal time to batch cook. You can freeze pastry cooked or uncooked. Cool completely before freezing.	**Uncooked:** Freeze blocks of pastry layered with wax paper, then wrapped in plastic wrap. **Cooked:** Freeze pies and tarts wrapped in wax paper and a double layer of plastic wrap.	Uncooked pies and pastry for up to 3 months. Cooked pies and tarts for up to 3 months.	Bake uncooked tart shells and pastries from frozen in the oven at 400°F (200°C), for 15 minutes. Thaw cooked pies and tarts overnight in the refrigerator, then bake at 350°F (180°C), for about 30 minutes, or until piping hot.

Tips for freezing

Follow these guidelines to prevent loss of quality, texture, taste, color, or nutrients, but never refreeze anything that has been frozen before—there is a high risk of bacteria multiplying in the thawing process before refreezing.

The fresher the food is when it goes in the freezer, the better it will be when it comes out. If you are aware of this when planning your shopping and cooking, you'll preserve the quality of the food.

Plan ahead when making big batches (doubling or tripling your recipe) as most dishes only freeze for up to 3 months, and you don't want too much of one dish.

Package the food in sensible amounts to prevent wastage—you should not refreeze after thawing. For soups, allow about 1 cup per person and avoid portion sizes larger than 2 cups. It's advisable to freeze in different portion sizes, too, to suit your requirements—larger portions for family meals and single-sized portions for when you are home alone and don't want to cook.

Label your containers so you know what's what and how long it has been frozen for. You can also use colored bags or boxes and develop a coding system for yourself.

To save space once foods are frozen, they can be removed from their solid containers and re-packed tightly in foil, plastic wrap, or resealable freezer bags. Foods will freeze quicker if you leave plenty of room around them or store them in the bottom of the freezer, where it is coldest.

Remember to rotate things in the freezer so everything gets used in time. It's first in, first out!

Avoid freezing...

Cream cheese or cottage cheese will separate or become watery, as will cream, unless it has been lightly whipped first.

Mayonnaise and hollandaise sauce will also separate when they are defrosted.

Fatty foods become fattier, and eventually turn rancid.

Salad ingredients such as cucumber, lettuce, celery, and tomatoes turn to water once defrosted.

If you are unsure whether something will freeze well, test a small amount first.

Once frozen, you can repackage ice cubes in a larger container to free up your trays.

7

Freezer packaging

The right packaging will protect your food so it keeps for longer. Remember to label packages, including portion sizes and packaging and expiration dates.

PACKAGING	BEST FOR	HOW TO USE
PLASTIC CONTAINERS Use ones that are durable so they don't become brittle and crack at low temperatures. They are available in all shapes and sizes and are easy to label and reuse.	Rigid plastic containers can be used to freeze all types of foods. They are especially good for bulky dishes that include a lot of sauce, such as casseroles, stews, and curries.	Let the food cool before filling the container and freezing. The plastic container can be placed in the refrigerator when it is time to defrost.
ICE CUBE TRAYS Freezing sauces and stocks in small portions allows you to use a large batch over time.	Ideal for freezing small amounts of sauce or stock. You could also use them to freeze leftover red wine, which you can then add to gravies or sauces.	Carefully fill with the liquid, leaving a little room for it to expand. Freeze when completely cool. Once frozen, transfer the cubes to plastic freezer bags or plastic containers and seal (otherwise the food will get freezer burn).
FOIL TRAYS These are a good choice if freezing foods for a few months. Use heavy-duty aluminum ones.	Most foods can be frozen in foil trays, but they are particularly useful for oven bakes as they are both ovenproof and freezerproof.	You can cook, freeze, and reheat foil trays in the oven. As different communities have varying recycling guidelines, check within your community to see if these foil trays are recyclable.
FOIL Foil can be used to create your own container, especially if you have a limited collection of ovenware.	This is best for recipes you can cook in the oven, including lasagnas, potato-topped pies, gratins, and roasts.	Double-line an ovenproof dish with foil, then fill with the food for cooking. Cook as per the recipe, let stand to cool, then freeze. Once frozen, lift out the foil dish and either wrap well in plastic wrap, or cover with a large freezer bag. Seal, and return to the freezer.

PACKAGING		BEST FOR	HOW TO USE
	BAGS FOR LIQUID You can store liquids in plastic bags by freezing them first in a rigid plastic container. These are excellent if you need to save containers and space.	Soups, sauces, ragùs, curries, and stews.	Line a plastic container with a freezerproof bag, then fill with stock, soup, or sauce and seal well, leaving some room for the contents to expand. Freeze until solid, then remove the container and stack the solid bag.
	PLASTIC FREEZER BAGS Freezer bags are very versatile for freezing. They need to be strong, leakproof, and resistant to moisture.	Most foods can be stored in polyethylene freezer bags. Bags with a built-in seal are ideal for all sauces and stews, and blanched vegetables.	Allow the food to cool completely before transferring to a freezer bag and storing in the freezer.

A guide to symbols

The recipes in this book are accompanied by symbols that alert you to important information.

Tells you how many people the recipe serves, or the quantity.

Indicates how much time you will need to prepare and cook a dish. Next to this symbol you will also find out if additional time is required for such things as marinating, standing, or cooling. You will have to read the recipe to find out exactly how much extra time is needed.

Points out that dish has nutritional benefits, such as low fat or low GI (Glycemic Index).

This important alert refers to preparation work that must be done before you can begin to cook the recipe. For example, you may need to soak some beans overnight.

This denotes that special equipment is required, such as an ovenproof pot or skewers. Where possible, alternatives are given.

Spicy

Chile beef and bean soup
page 36

Chicken and chile burgers
page 120

Chicken korma page 66

Curried vegetable pies page 186

Vegetable curry page 52

Garlic and chile chicken with honey sweet potato page 74

Stuffed eggplants page 128

Chili con carne page 94

Pan-fried lamb with green chiles page 118

Thai crab cakes page 126

Chickpea curry with cardamom page 58

Black bean and coconut soup page 40

Chicken jalfrezi page 72

Couscous royale page 50

Caribbean stew with allspice and ginger page 64

Spicy beef pies page 170

Comfort

Split pea and bacon soup
page 38

Lamb and pea pie page 176

Beef ragù page 194

Shepherd's Pie page 140

Chicken and sweet corn pie page 174

**Beef and celery root casserole
with stout and anchovies** page 88

Fish and leek pie page 178

Sausages with lima beans
page 100

Moussaka page 136

Leek and potato soup page 28

Haddock with cheese sauce
page 152

Cheese and onion pie page 182

**Cheesy potato and mushroom
gratin** page 146

Chicken and cornmeal cobbler
page 70

Pork with rice and tomatoes
page 84

Healthy

Mixed bean medley page 48

Lamb daube page 82

Thick vegetable soup page 32

Chunky ratatouille page 54

Pork and bean casserole
page 90

Shepherdless pie page 150

**Garlic and chile chicken with
honey sweet potato** page 74

**Lamb, spinach, and chickpea
hotpot** page 102

Braised turkey with vegetables page 60

Vegetarian moussaka page 148

Chicken and chile burgers
page 120

Bean and rosemary soup
page 30

Chickpea curry with cardamom
page 58

**Pearl barley and borlotti bean
one-pot** page 56

Mixed fish kebabs page 116

Great for a crowd

Lamb and eggplant ragù
page 196

Lamb daube page 82

Game stew page 104

Beef shank with Marsala
page 76

Pork with fennel and mustard
page 78

Spiced sausage cassoulet
page 96

Beef stew with orange and bay leaves page 98

Spanish meatballs page 110

Vegetarian leek and mushroom lasagna page 142

Pork goulash page 80

Chili con carne page 94

Pork and bean casserole
page 90

Beef and celery root casserole with stout and anchovies page 88

Chicken and cornmeal cobbler page 70

Vegetarian

Cheesy potato and mushroom gratin page 146

Mixed mushroom and walnut tart page 190

Calzone with peppers, capers, and olives page 166

Tomato soup page 26

Shepherdless pie page 150

Vegetarian moussaka page 148

Stuffed eggplants page 128

Eggplant parmigiana page 134

Gruyère, potato, and thyme tartlets page 188

Chunky ratatouille page 54

Vegetarian leek and mushroom lasagna page 142

Thick vegetable soup page 32

Vegetable curry page 52

Swiss chard and Gruyère cheese tart page 168

Mushroom and ricotta pies with red pepper pesto page 184

Pearl barley and borlotti bean one-pot page 56

Make vegetable stock

Stocks can be made in large quantities and then frozen for up to 6 months. They are invaluable ingredients for soups, risottos, casseroles, and more.

1 Place chopped carrots, celery, onion, and a leek into a large deep pan. Add peppercorns, parsley, and bay leaves. Cover with water and bring to a boil. Reduce the heat and simmer for up to 1 hour.

2 Ladle through a fine sieve, pressing the vegetables against the sieve to extract any extra liquid. Season to taste with salt and freshly ground black pepper. Let cool and refrigerate for up to 2 days, or freeze.

Make chicken stock

Simmering the remains of your roast chicken with a few vegetables and herbs will produce a light golden stock that you can freeze for up to 6 months.

1 Add either raw chicken bones or roasted chicken bones into a large deep pan with chopped carrots, celery, onions, and a bouquet garni of fresh herbs of your choice.

2 Cover with water, and bring to a boil. Reduce the heat and simmer for 1–3 hours, skimming frequently. Ladle through a fine sieve and season to taste. Let cool and refrigerate for up to 2 days, or freeze.

Make beef stock

Using beef bones will produce a richer and darker stock than chicken, particularly if you roast the bones first. Freeze the stock for up to 6 months.

1 Use either leftover rib bones from a roast, or purchase a bag of beef bones from your butcher. Put the bones in a large roasting pan, add a handful of vegetables such as carrots, celery, and onion, and season. Roast for 30 minutes.

2 Add the roasted bones and vegetables to a large deep pan with some fresh sprigs of thyme, rosemary, or another woody herb of your choice, then pour in enough cold water to cover the contents of the pan completely.

3 Bring to a boil, then reduce to a gentle simmer. Cook with the lid half-on for about 1 hour, carefully skimming off any fat that comes to the top of the pan, if necessary.

4 Remove the bones from the pan and discard, then strain the liquid through a fine sieve into a large storage container, and season to taste. Let cool and refrigerate for up to 2 days, or freeze.

Tomato soup

This classic is a thick, warming soup.

INGREDIENTS

3 tbsp olive oil

3 onions, finely chopped

4 garlic cloves, finely chopped

30 tomatoes (about 3lb/1.35kg), quartered

sea salt and freshly ground black pepper

2 tsp superfine sugar (optional)

1 tbsp tomato paste or purée

$2^1/_2$ cups hot vegetable stock

$^2/_3$ cup heavy cream (optional), to serve

METHOD

1 Heat the oil in a soup pot, add the onions, and cook over low heat for 10 minutes, stirring so the onions don't burn. Stir in the garlic and tomatoes and season with salt and pepper. Add the sugar (if using) and tomato paste or purée, stir, and then cook over very low heat for 30 minutes.

2 Pour in the stock, bring to a boil, then lower the heat and simmer for 10 minutes. Transfer to a blender or food processor and process until smooth.

3 Return the soup to the soup pot, stir in the cream (if using), and heat until piping hot. Taste and season again if needed.

FREEZING INSTRUCTIONS Omit the cream if freezing, as it may separate. Let the soup stand to cool completely, then freeze in a sealable freezerproof container for up to 3 months. To serve, defrost in the refrigerator overnight, then reheat gently in a pan. Stir in the cream (if using) when almost hot, and heat through until piping hot.

serves 8

**prep 15 mins
• cook 50 mins**

healthy option

**blender or food
processor**

Leek and potato soup

Potatoes give this comforting soup body, while leeks lend a silky texture.

INGREDIENTS

2 tbsp olive oil

2 onions, finely chopped

sea salt and freshly ground black pepper

3 garlic cloves, finely chopped

6 sage leaves, finely chopped

2lb (900g) leeks, cleaned and finely sliced

5 cups hot vegetable stock

2lb (900g) potatoes, roughly chopped

$^2/_3$ cup heavy cream, to serve

METHOD

1 Heat the oil in a large pan, add the onions, and cook over low heat for 6–8 minutes, or until soft. Season with salt and pepper, then stir in the garlic and sage. Add the leeks and stir well, then cook over low heat for 10 minutes or until the leeks start to soften.

2 Pour in the stock, bring to a boil, then add the potatoes and simmer for about 20 minutes, or until soft. Transfer to a food processor or blender and process until blended and smooth.

3 Return the soup to the pan, stir in the cream, and heat until piping hot. Taste and season with salt and pepper if needed.

FREEZING INSTRUCTIONS Omit the cream if freezing as it may separate. Let stand to cool completely, then freeze in a sealable freezerproof container for up to 3 months. To serve, defrost in the refrigerator overnight, then reheat gently in a pan, stir in the cream when almost hot, and heat through until piping hot.

serves 8

prep 15 mins
• cook 40 mins

blender or
food processor

Bean and rosemary soup

Simple, filling soups like this one are great to have on standby in the freezer.

INGREDIENTS

2 tbsp olive oil, plus a little extra (according to taste)
2 onions, finely chopped
sea salt and freshly ground black pepper
1 tbsp finely chopped rosemary leaves
a few sage leaves, finely chopped
4 celery stalks, finely chopped
3 garlic cloves, finely chopped
2 tbsp tomato paste or purée
2 x 14oz (400g) cans cannellini beans
4 cups hot chicken stock
2lb (2.5kg) potatoes, cut into $^{1}/_{2}$in (1cm) cubes

METHOD

1 Heat the oil in a large saucepan, add the onions, and cook over low heat for 6–8 minutes or until soft. Season well with salt and pepper, then stir in the rosemary, sage, celery, and garlic and cook over very low heat, stirring occasionally, for 10 minutes.

2 Stir through the tomato purée and beans, add a little more olive oil if you wish, and cook gently for 5 minutes. Pour in the stock, bring to a boil, then add the potatoes and simmer gently for about 15 minutes, or until cooked. Taste and season again with salt and pepper if needed.

FREEZING INSTRUCTIONS Let stand to cool completely, then freeze in a sealable freezerproof container for up to 3 months. To serve, defrost in the refrigerator overnight, then reheat gently in a saucepan until piping hot. Add a little hot water or hot stock if the soup is too thick. Alternatively, reheat in a microwave on medium for 2–3 minutes, then stir and heat for 2–3 minutes more, or until piping hot. Let stand for 5 minutes before serving.

serves 8

prep 15 mins
• cook 40 mins

healthy option

Thick vegetable soup

This chunky soup will warm you up in the winter.

INGREDIENTS
2 tbsp olive oil
2 onions, finely chopped
sea salt and freshly ground black pepper
4 garlic cloves, finely chopped
1 tbsp finely chopped rosemary leaves
4 celery stalks, finely chopped
4 carrots, finely chopped
4 zucchini, finely chopped
1 x 28oz (800g) can whole tomatoes, chopped
4 cups hot vegetable stock
handful of flat-leaf parsley, finely chopped

METHOD

1 Heat the oil in a large pan, add the onions, and cook over low heat for 6–8 minutes, or until soft. Season with salt and pepper, then add the garlic, rosemary, celery, and carrots and cook over low heat, stirring occasionally, for 10 minutes.

2 Add the zucchini and cook for 5 minutes, then stir in the tomatoes and mash with the back of a fork. Add the stock, bring to a boil, then reduce to a simmer and cook for 20 minutes. Season with salt and pepper, then stir in the parsley.

FREEZING INSTRUCTIONS Let stand to cool completely, then freeze in a sealable freezerproof container for up to 3 months. To serve, defrost in the refrigerator overnight, then reheat gently in a saucepan until piping hot. Add a little hot water or hot stock if the soup is too thick. Alternatively, reheat in a microwave on medium for 2–3 minutes, then stir and heat for 2–3 minutes more, or until piping hot. Let stand for 5 minutes before serving.

serves 8

prep 15 mins
• cook 45 mins

healthy option

Chestnut and bacon soup

The crunchy texture and nutty flavor of this soup is very satisfying.

INGREDIENTS

2 tbsp olive oil
2 onions, finely chopped
9oz (250g) bacon or pancetta, chopped into
 bite-sized pieces
4 garlic cloves, finely chopped
1 tbsp rosemary leaves, finely chopped
sea salt and freshly ground black pepper
3 x 7oz (200g) packs roasted chestnuts, chopped
4 cups hot chicken stock

METHOD

1 Heat the oil in a large pan, add the onions, and cook over low heat for 5–8 minutes or until soft. Add the bacon or pancetta and cook for 5 minutes or until crispy. Stir in the garlic and rosemary, then season with salt and pepper.

2 Stir in the chestnuts, pour in the stock, and bring to a boil. Lower the heat and simmer for 15–20 minutes. Using a slotted spoon, remove a few spoonfuls of the bacon and set aside. Purée the rest of the soup in a food processor or blender.

3 Return the soup to the pan, add the reserved bacon pieces and heat through until piping hot, adding a little hot water if the soup is too thick. Season again with salt and pepper if needed. Serve with a drizzle of extra virgin olive oil.

FREEZING INSTRUCTIONS Let stand to cool completely, then transfer to a sealable freezerproof container, making sure the bacon pieces are covered by liquid. Freeze for up to 3 months. To serve, defrost overnight in the refrigerator, then reheat gently in a saucepan until piping hot. Add a little hot water if the soup is too thick. Alternatively, reheat in a microwave on medium for 2–3 minutes, then stir and heat for 2–3 minutes more, or until piping hot. Let stand for 5 minutes. Serve with a drizzle of extra virgin olive oil.

serves 8

prep 15 mins
• cook 30 mins

blender or
food processor

Chile beef and bean soup

Spicy Tex-Mex style flavors are sure to make this soup a favorite.

INGREDIENTS

2 tbsp olive oil
2 onions, finely chopped
sea salt and freshly ground black pepper
2 red peppers, seeded and finely chopped
2–3 red chiles, seeded and finely chopped
1¼lb (550g) beef stew meat, cut into 1in (2.5cm) cubes
1 tbsp all-purpose flour
8 cups hot beef stock
2 x 14oz (400g) cans kidney beans, drained
handful of flat-leaf parsley, finely chopped, to serve

METHOD

1 Heat the oil in a large heavy-based saucepan, add the onions, and cook over low heat for about 6–8 minutes or until soft. Season with salt and pepper, then stir in the peppers and chiles and cook for 5 minutes. Add the meat and cook, stirring frequently, for 5–10 minutes until it begins to brown all over.

2 Sprinkle in the flour, stir well, then cook for 2 minutes. Add the stock, bring to a boil, then cover with a lid and reduce to a simmer. Cook for 1½ hours or until the meat is tender. Add the kidney beans and cook for 10 minutes more, then season to taste with salt and pepper. Stir in the parsley and serve.

FREEZING INSTRUCTIONS Let stand to cool completely, then transfer to a sealable freezerproof container, making sure the meat is covered by liquid (add a little more cold stock if it isn't). Freeze for up to 3 months. To serve, defrost overnight in the refrigerator, then reheat gently in a saucepan at a low simmer until piping hot. Add a little hot water if the soup is too thick. Alternatively, reheat in a microwave on medium for 2–3 minutes, then stir and heat for 2–3 minutes more, or until piping hot. Let stand for 5 minutes. Stir in some parsley and serve.

serves 8

prep 20 mins
• cook 2 hrs

Split pea and bacon soup

This thick soup is a pleasure to eat. The bacon adds flavor, but can be left out for vegetarians.

INGREDIENTS

2 tbsp olive oil

15oz (425g) bacon or pancetta, chopped into
   bite-sized pieces

2 onions, finely chopped

sea salt and freshly ground black pepper

4 celery stalks, finely chopped

4 carrots, finely chopped

1¼lb (550g) yellow split peas

6 cups hot vegetable stock

METHOD

1 Heat half the oil in a large heavy-based saucepan, add the bacon or pancetta, and cook over medium heat, stirring occasionally, for 5 minutes or until crispy. Remove with a slotted spoon and set aside. Heat the remaining oil in the pan, add the onions, and cook over low heat for 6–8 minutes until soft. Season with salt and pepper, then add the celery and carrots and cook over low heat for 5 minutes.

2 Add the peas and stock and slowly bring to a boil. Cover with a lid, reduce to a simmer, and cook for 2 hours or until the peas are tender. Check occasionally and add hot water if the soup begins to look too thick. Transfer the soup to a food processor or blender and process until smooth and blended.

3 Return the soup to the pan and add the reserved bacon or pancetta. Heat through until piping hot. Taste and season with salt and pepper if needed.

FREEZING INSTRUCTIONS Let stand to cool completely, then transfer to a sealable freezerproof container, making sure the bacon pieces are covered by liquid. Freeze for up to 3 months. To serve, defrost overnight in the refrigerator, then reheat the soup in a saucepan until piping hot, adding a little hot water if the soup is too thick. Alternatively, reheat in a microwave on medium for 2–3 minutes, then stir and heat for 2–3 minutes more, or until piping hot. Let stand for 5 minutes before serving.

serves 8

prep 15 mins
• cook 2 hrs
20 mins

blender or
food processor

Black bean and coconut soup

Exotic flavors make this soup a great introduction to a spicy main course.

INGREDIENTS
2 tbsp olive oil
2 red onions, finely chopped
2 bay leaves
sea salt and freshly ground black pepper
4 garlic cloves, finely chopped
2 tsp ground cumin
2 tsp ground coriander
1 tsp chili powder
2 x 14oz (400g) cans drained black beans
4 cups hot vegetable stock
1 x 14oz (400ml) can coconut milk
flour tortillas, to serve

METHOD
1 Heat the oil in a saucepan, add the onions and bay leaves, and cook over low heat for 6–8 minutes until the onions soften. Season with salt and pepper. Stir in the garlic, cumin, coriander, and chili powder and cook for a few seconds.

2 Stir in the black beans, then pour in the stock and coconut milk. Bring to a boil, then reduce to a simmer and cook for 15–20 minutes. Remove the bay leaves and discard, then transfer the soup to a food processor or blender and pulse a couple of times so some of the beans are puréed and some remain whole.

3 Return the soup to the pan and heat through, stirring occasionally. Add a little more stock if it is too thick. Taste and season again with salt and pepper if needed.

FREEZING INSTRUCTIONS Let stand to cool completely, then freeze in a sealable freezerproof container for up to 3 months. To serve, defrost in the refrigerator overnight, then reheat gently in a saucepan until piping hot. Alternatively, reheat in a microwave on medium for 2–3 minutes, then stir and heat for 2–3 minutes more, or until piping hot. Let stand for 5 minutes before serving.

serves 8

prep 15 mins
• cook 30 mins

blender or
food processor

Chunky minestrone soup

This flavorful combination of pasta and vegetables makes a great meal for a rainy day.

INGREDIENTS

2 tbsp olive oil
2 onions, finely chopped
3 garlic cloves, finely chopped
4 celery stalks, finely chopped
4 carrots, finely chopped
9oz (250g) pancetta, cut into small cubes
handful of flat-leaf parsley, finely chopped
handful of fresh sage leaves, finely chopped
2 tbsp tomato paste or purée

1 x 28oz (800g) can chopped tomatoes
2 x 14oz (400g) cans borlotti or cranberry
   beans, drained, rinsed, and drained again
sea salt and freshly ground black pepper
2 cups hot chicken stock
8oz (225g) fresh or frozen peas
10oz (300g) green beans, cut into thirds
10oz (300g) small pasta shapes such as fusilli
grated Parmesan cheese, to serve

METHOD

1 Heat the oil in a heavy-based pan, add the onions, and cook over low heat for 6–8 minutes or until soft. Add the garlic, celery, and carrots and continue to cook, stirring, for 10 minutes, until soft. Stir in the pancetta and cook for 5 minutes or until browned.

2 Add the herbs, tomato paste, tomatoes, and beans and stir to combine. Season with salt and pepper, then pour in the stock. Bring to a boil, then cover with a lid and simmer for 40 minutes. Add the peas and beans for the last 5 minutes of cooking.

3 Add the pasta and simmer until the pasta is *al dente* and the soup is piping hot. Taste and season again if needed, top with the Parmesan cheese, and serve.

FREEZING INSTRUCTIONS Let stand to cool completely, then transfer to a sealable freezerproof container, making sure the pancetta and pasta are completely immersed in liquid (add a little cooled stock if they aren't). Freeze for up to 3 months. To serve, defrost in the refrigerator overnight, then gently reheat the soup in a saucepan until piping hot. Serve with a sprinkle of grated Parmesan cheese.

serves 8

prep 25 mins
• cook 1 hr

healthy option

Peel and chop garlic

Garlic is essential to many recipes and peeling it is easy once you know how. The finer you chop garlic, the more flavor you'll release.

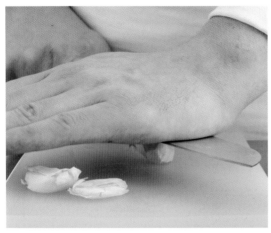

1 Lay each garlic clove flat on a cutting board. Place the side of a chef's knife blade on it. Press firmly on the flat of the blade to break the garlic skin, then discard it.

2 Chop the garlic roughly, then sprinkle with a little salt to prevent it from sticking to the knife. Gather the pieces into a pile and chop again crosswise for finer pieces.

Chop onion

Once an onion is halved, it can be sliced or diced. This technique is for quick dicing, which helps prevent your eyes from watering.

1 Peel the onion and cut it in half, then lay the cut side down. Slice down through the layers vertically, cutting up to, but not through, the root end.

2 Cut across the vertical slices to produce even dice. Use the root to hold the onion steady, then discard when the onion is diced.

Chop herbs

Chop fresh herbs just before using to release their flavor and aroma. You may wish to reserve a small amount to use as a garnish for the finished dish.

1 To chop leaves (a mixture or a single variety as the basil leaves above), strip them from their stems and gather them together in a tight pile. If using large-leafed herbs, layer them and roll them up.

2 Using a large, sharp chef's knife, chop through the pile of herbs with a steady rocking motion. Turn the pile 90° as you work, chopping until you have the size you want.

Seed and cut chiles

Chiles contain capsaicin, a pungent compound that is a strong irritant to skin and mucus membranes. Always wash your hands after handling chiles.

1 Cut the chile in half lengthwise. Using the tip of your knife or a small spoon, scrape out and discard the seeds, ribs, and stem.

2 Flatten each chile half and slice into strips. To dice, hold the strips firmly together, and slice crosswise to make equal-sized pieces.

Mixed bean medley

Wholesome and tasty, this one-pot meal makes a hearty dinner.

INGREDIENTS

1 tbsp olive oil
1 onion, finely chopped
sea salt and freshly ground black pepper
2 garlic cloves, finely chopped
4 thick bacon slices, cut crosswise into $^1/_2$in (.6cm)
  strips, or 4$^1/_2$oz (125g) pancetta, cut into small cubes
pinch of crushed hot pepper flakes
2 tsp dried oregano
1 x 15oz (425g) can mixed beans, drained and rinsed
1$^3/_4$ cups pale ale
3$^3/_4$ cups hot vegetable stock

METHOD

1 Heat the oil in a large deep-sided frying pan over low heat. Add the onion and a pinch of salt, and cook gently for about 5 minutes. Stir in the garlic, and cook for about 30 seconds.

2 Increase the heat slightly, and add the bacon or pancetta. Cook for about 5 minutes, or until golden. Drain off excess fat, if needed. Sprinkle in the pepper flakes and oregano, and stir in the beans.

3 Pour in the ale, bring to a boil, and cook over high heat for 5 minutes. Add the stock, reduce the heat slightly, and simmer gently for 20–25 minutes, stirring occasionally, until the mixture thickens. Season with salt and pepper. Serve hot.

FREEZING INSTRUCTIONS Let stand to cool completely, then freeze in a sealable freezerproof container for up to 3 months. To serve, defrost in the refrigerator overnight, then reheat gently in a saucepan, adding water as needed, until piping hot. Alternatively, reheat in a microwave on medium for 2–3 minutes, then stir and heat for 2–3 minutes more, or until piping hot. Let stand for 5 minutes before serving.

GOOD WITH Fresh crusty bread to mop up the flavorful gravy.

serves 4

prep 10 mins
• cook 40 mins

healthy option

Couscous royale

This richly spiced dish makes a colorful Moroccan feast.

INGREDIENTS

2 tbsp olive oil

1lb 5oz (600g) boneless leg of lamb, cut into bite-sized chunks

6 chicken legs, about 3lb 3oz (1.5kg)

1 eggplant, cut into 1in (2.5cm) pieces

1 red bell pepper, seeded and diced

1 large red onion, sliced

2 garlic cloves, finely chopped

4 tsp harissa (hot Moroccan chile paste)

1 tbsp sweet paprika

1 tsp ground turmeric

2 medium zucchini, sliced

1 cup chicken stock

1 x 15oz (420g) can chickpeas, rinsed and drained

1 x 14.5oz (400g) can chopped tomatoes

6oz (175g) chorizo, thickly sliced

salt and freshly ground black pepper

large sprig of thyme

1 bay leaf

2¼ cups couscous

chopped cilantro, to garnish

METHOD

1 Heat the oil in the casserole over medium-high heat. Add the lamb and chicken and cook, turning occasionally, about 6 minutes. Transfer to paper towels to drain.

2 Add the eggplant, red pepper, onion, and garlic to the casserole and cook, stirring occasionally, about 4 minutes. Stir in the harissa, paprika, and turmeric and cook for 1 minute.

3 Return the lamb and chicken to the casserole. Add the zucchini, stock, beans, tomatoes, and chorizo and season with salt and pepper. Bring to a boil. Reduce the heat to low and cover. Simmer about 1 hour, or until the meats are tender.

4 Strain the mixture in a colander set over a wide skillet. Transfer the meat and vegetables to a platter and cover to keep warm. Boil the strained liquid over high heat for about 5 minutes, or until slightly reduced. Season with salt and pepper.

5 Bring 3 cups water and ½ teaspoon salt to a boil in a large saucepan. Stir in the couscous and remove from the heat. Cover and let stand until the couscous is tender, about 5 minutes. Stir the meats and vegetables into the couscous. Pour the sauce on top and sprinkle with the cilantro.

FREEZING INSTRUCTIONS Omit the couscous if freezing. Prepare the recipe to the end of Step 3, then let stand to cool. Transfer to a sealable freezerproof container, making sure the meat is completely covered by the sauce (add stock if needed), and freeze for up to 2 months. To thaw, defrost overnight in the refrigerator. To serve, prepare the couscous according to its instructions and set aside. Reheat the meat mixture in a saucepan, adding water as needed to prevent scorching, until piping hot. Stir through the couscous and serve sprinkled with some chopped cilantro.

serves 6

prep 10 mins
• cook 1 hr
20 mins

large flameproof
casserole

Vegetable curry

Indians consider cardamom, cloves, coriander, and cumin seeds to be "warming spices" that heat the body from within, making this an excellent winter dish.

INGREDIENTS

1/4 cup vegetable oil

10oz (300g) red-skinned potatoes, diced

5 green cardamom pods, crushed

3 whole cloves

1 cinnamon stick, broken in half

2 tsp cumin seeds

1 onion, finely chopped

2 tsp peeled and grated fresh ginger

2 large garlic cloves, crushed

1 1/2 tsp ground turmeric

1 tsp ground coriander

salt and freshly ground black pepper

1 x 14.5oz (411g) can chopped tomatoes

pinch of sugar

2 carrots, diced

2 fresh green chiles, seeded (optional) and sliced into thin rounds

1 cup sliced Savoy or green cabbage

1 cup cauliflower florets

1 cup thawed frozen peas

2 tbsp chopped cilantro

toasted sliced almonds, to garnish

METHOD

1 Heat the oil in a large deep frying pan over high heat. Add the potatoes and cook, stirring often, for 5 minutes, or until golden brown. Using a slotted spoon, transfer to paper towels to drain.

2 Reduce the heat to medium. Add the cardamom pods, cloves, cinnamon, and cumin seeds and stir until the spices are very fragrant. Add the onion and cook, stirring often, for about 5 minutes, or until softened. Add the ginger, garlic, turmeric, and coriander, and season with salt and pepper. Stir for 1 minute.

3 Stir in the tomatoes with their juices and add the sugar. Return the potatoes to the pan, add the carrots, chiles, and 1 cup of water, and bring to a boil, stirring often. Reduce the heat to low. Simmer, stirring occasionally, for 15 minutes, or until the carrots are just tender, adding a little more water if needed.

4 Stir in the cabbage, cauliflower, and peas. Return the heat to medium and simmer for about 10 minutes, or until the vegetables are tender. Stir in the cilantro and season again. Remove and discard the cardamom pods and cloves. Transfer to a serving bowl, sprinkle with almonds, and serve hot.

FREEZING INSTRUCTIONS Let stand to cool completely, then transfer to a sealable freezerproof container, making sure the vegetables are covered by the sauce. Freeze for up to 3 months. To serve, defrost in the refrigerator overnight, then reheat in a saucepan, adding water if needed, until piping hot. Alternatively, reheat in a microwave on medium for 2–3 minutes, then stir and heat for 2–3 minutes more, or until piping hot.

GOOD WITH Lots of basmati rice or naan bread.

serves 4–6

prep 20 mins
• cook 35–45 mins

Chunky ratatouille

This French classic is full of tasty vegetables and is an excellent healthy choice.

INGREDIENTS
1 tbsp olive oil
1 onion, finely chopped
sea salt and freshly ground black pepper
1 bay leaf
2 garlic cloves, thinly sliced
1–2 tsp dried oregano
pinch of fennel seeds
1 eggplant, cut into chunks
$\frac{1}{2}$ cup dry red wine
$\frac{2}{3}$ cup tomato juice
2 small zucchini, cut into chunks
3 tomatoes, coarsely chopped
large handful of Swiss chard leaves
freshly chopped flat-leaf parsley leaves, for garnish

METHOD
1 Heat the oil in a large saucepan over low heat. Add the onion, a pinch of salt, and the bay leaf, and cook for about 5 minutes or until the onion is soft.

2 Add the garlic, oregano, fennel seeds, eggplant, and wine. Let bubble for a minute, then add the tomato juice. Cook for about 10 minutes, or until the eggplant is soft.

3 Now add the zucchini and chopped tomatoes, and cook for 5–10 minutes longer. Stir in the Swiss chard, and cook until all the vegetables are tender. Taste, and season with salt and pepper if needed. Garnish with the parsley, and serve hot.

FREEZING INSTRUCTIONS Let stand to cool completely, then transfer to a sealable freezerproof container, making sure the Swiss chard is immersed in liquid. Freeze for up to 3 months. To serve, defrost in the refrigerator overnight, then reheat gently in a saucepan, adding hot stock if needed, until piping hot. Garnish with chopped parsley to serve.

GOOD WITH Fluffy rice or some fresh crusty bread and a salad.

serves 4

prep 15 mins
• cook 30 mins

healthy option

Pearl barley and borlotti bean one-pot

A warm, comforting dish for a winter day.

INGREDIENTS

1 tbsp olive oil
1 onion, finely chopped
sea salt and freshly ground
    black pepper
$\frac{1}{2}$ cup (125g) dry red wine
$1\frac{1}{2}$ cups (6oz/175g) pearl barley
1 x 15oz (425g) can borlotti
    beans, drained and rinsed
1 x 14oz (400g) can diced tomatoes,
    with juices
4 cups (1.1 liters) hot vegetable stock
hot chili oil, to serve (optional)

METHOD

1 Heat the oil in a large heavy saucepan over low heat. Add the onion and a pinch of salt, and cook gently for 5 minutes, or until soft. Increase the heat, pour in the wine, and bubble for about 5 minutes.

2 Reduce the heat to low, add the pearl barley, and stir well until it has absorbed all the liquid. Stir in the beans, tomatoes, and hot stock. Return to a boil, and continue boiling for 5 minutes.

3 Reduce the heat to low once again, season well with salt and pepper, and gently simmer for 25–40 minutes until the pearl barley is cooked and all the stock has been absorbed. If the mixture starts to dry out, add a little hot water. Drizzle with a splash of chili oil (optional) and serve hot.

FREEZING INSTRUCTIONS Let stand to cool, then freeze in a sealable freezerproof container for up to 3 months. To serve, defrost in the refrigerator overnight, then reheat in a saucepan, adding hot water if needed. Simmer gently for 15–20 minutes, or until piping hot. Alternatively, reheat in a microwave, adding water if the consistency is too thick, on medium for 2–3 minutes, then stir and heat for 2–3 minutes more, or until piping hot. Let stand for 5 minutes. Serve with a drizzle of chili oil, if using.

GOOD WITH Fresh crusty bread.

serves 4

prep 10 mins
• cook 1 hr

healthy option

Chickpea curry with cardamom

This hearty vegetarian dish satisfies for lunch or dinner.

INGREDIENTS

1 tbsp vegetable oil
1 onion, finely chopped
sea salt and freshly ground black pepper
1 tsp cumin seeds
1 tsp turmeric
1 tsp ground coriander
6 green cardamom pods, lightly crushed
1 x 15$\frac{1}{2}$oz (440g) can chickpeas, drained and rinsed
1 x 14oz (400g) can diced tomatoes, with juices
1–2 tsp garam masala
1 tsp hot chili powder, or more to taste

METHOD

1 Heat the oil in a large heavy saucepan over low heat. Add the onion and a pinch of salt, and cook gently for about 5 minutes until soft. Stir in the cumin seeds, turmeric, coriander, and cardamom, and continue cooking for about 5 minutes until fragrant.

2 Add the chickpeas to the pan, and stir well, crushing them very slightly with the back of a wooden spoon. Stir in the tomatoes, including any juices, then fill the empty can with water and add this as well. Sprinkle in the garam masala and chili powder, and bring to a boil. Reduce the heat to low, and simmer gently for about 20 minutes, or until the sauce begins to thicken. Season with salt and pepper. Serve hot.

FREEZING INSTRUCTIONS Let stand to cool completely, then transfer to a sealable freezerproof container and freeze for up to 3 months. To serve, defrost in the refrigerator overnight, then reheat in a saucepan, adding hot water if needed. Simmer gently until piping hot. Alternatively, reheat in a microwave, adding hot water if needed, on medium for 2–3 minutes, then stir and heat for 2–3 minutes more, or until piping hot.

GOOD WITH Naan bread or basmati rice.

serves 4

prep 10 mins
• cook 30 mins

healthy option

Braised turkey with vegetables

Fresh flavors of lemon and tarragon enliven this recipe.

INGREDIENTS
2 tbsp olive oil
1 tbsp butter
4 turkey breast fillets (skin on)
sea salt and freshly ground black pepper
2 onions, sliced
2 carrots, sliced
1 fennel bulb, sliced
a few fresh tarragon leaves, roughly chopped
2 cups hot chicken stock
handful of fresh flat-leaf parsley, finely chopped, to serve
zest of 1 lemon, grated, to serve

METHOD
1 Preheat the oven to 350°F (180°C). Heat the oil and butter in a large frying pan, season the turkey, then cook over medium heat, stirring occasionally, for 10 minutes, or until lightly browned all over. Transfer to a shallow casserole dish.

2 Add the vegetables and tarragon and season again. Pour stock almost to the top of the dish, but not enough to cover the ingredients. Cover with a lid and cook in the oven for 40 minutes, or until the turkey and vegetables are tender. Top with the parsley and lemon zest and serve with a pinch of pepper.

FREEZING INSTRUCTIONS Let stand to cool completely, then remove the turkey and slice the meat. Transfer to a sealable freezerproof container, making sure the turkey is well covered with the sauce (add a little more cold stock if it isn't). Freeze for up to 3 months. To serve, defrost in the refrigerator overnight, then reheat in a saucepan, adding hot water if needed. Simmer gently for 15–20 minutes, or until piping hot. Alternatively, reheat in a microwave on high for 3–4 minutes, then stir and heat for 3–4 minutes more, or until piping hot. Let stand for 5 minutes. Serve with chopped parsley and lemon zest.

GOOD WITH Mashed boiled new potatoes.

serves 8

prep 20 mins
• cook 40 mins

healthy option

Coq au vin

This quick version of the famous dish from Burgundy makes a delicious and hearty family lunch.

INGREDIENTS

3 tbsp butter
3 tbsp olive oil
2 large onions, diced
10 garlic cloves, chopped
10oz (300g) side pork, chopped (or bacon)
2 tbsp fresh thyme leaves
1lb 10oz (750g) button mushrooms
4 cups good red wine
4 cups hot chicken stock
2$\frac{1}{2}$lb (1.1kg) skinless chicken pieces
sea salt and freshly ground black pepper

METHOD

1 Heat the butter and oil in a large heavy-based pot over medium heat, add the onions, and cook for 5 minutes or until starting to soften. Add the garlic and side pork (or bacon) and cook for 5 minutes, stirring frequently. Add the thyme and mushrooms and cook for 2 minutes.

2 Pour in the wine, raise the heat, and allow to bubble for 5 minutes while the alcohol evaporates. Pour in the stock, bring to a boil, then add the chicken pieces. Combine well, bring to a boil again, then lower the heat and simmer for 25 minutes. Season with salt and pepper. Serve hot.

FREEZING INSTRUCTIONS Let stand to cool, then transfer to a sealable freezerproof container, making sure the chicken is completely covered by sauce. Freeze for up to 3 months. To serve, defrost overnight in the refrigerator, then transfer to a casserole dish, cover, and reheat in an oven preheated to 350°F (180°C) for about 25 minutes, or until piping hot. Add a little hot water or hot stock if the casserole starts to dry out.

GOOD WITH Parsley-buttered potatoes or fresh crusty French bread.

serves 8

prep 15 mins
• cook 40 mins

Caribbean stew with allspice and ginger

Scotch bonnet chiles are very fiery so use one or two depending on your taste.

INGREDIENTS

1–2 Scotch bonnet chiles, seeded
2 tsp allspice
handful of fresh thyme leaves
2 tsp tamarind paste
2in (5cm) fresh ginger, peeled and
    coarsely chopped
sea salt and freshly ground black pepper
3 tbsp olive oil

4 large skinless chicken breasts,
    cut into bite-sized pieces
1 tbsp all-purpose flour
5 cups hot chicken stock
4 bell peppers (a mix of colors),
    seeded and coarsely chopped
5 tomatoes, skinned and
    coarsely chopped

METHOD

1 Put the chiles, allspice, thyme, tamarind, ginger, and some salt and pepper into a food processor and pulse, turning the machine on and off, until the ingredients become a paste. Add a little of the oil and process again. Pour into a plastic bag, add the chicken, and squish together. Allow to marinate for 30 minutes (or overnight in the refrigerator).

2 Heat the remaining oil in a large cast-iron pot, add the chicken and paste, and cook, stirring often, over medium heat for 10 minutes or until the chicken is evenly browned. Stir in the flour, then add a little of the stock and stir to scrape up any crispy bits that are stuck to the bottom of the pot. Pour in the rest of the stock and keep stirring until the flour has dissolved.

3 Stir in the peppers and tomatoes and season well with salt and pepper. Bring to a boil, then reduce to a simmer and cook over low heat for 30 minutes or until the sauce has begun to thicken slightly. Taste and season again if needed.

FREEZING INSTRUCTIONS Let stand to cool completely, then transfer to a sealable freezerproof container, making sure the chicken is covered by sauce. Freeze for up to 3 months. To serve, defrost in the refrigerator overnight, then transfer to a casserole dish, cover, and reheat in an oven preheated to 350°F (180°C) for 30–40 minutes, or until piping hot. Add a little hot water or hot stock if the stew starts to dry out.

GOOD WITH Baked or mashed sweet potatoes.

serves 8

prep 30 mins,
plus marinating
• cook 30 mins

blender or food
processor
• large cast-iron
pan or
flameproof
casserole

Chicken korma

A mild curry popular in Indian restaurants, this is a fragrant and aromatic dish with a creamy sauce.

INGREDIENTS

4 tbsp vegetable oil or ghee (clarified butter)

8 skinless, boneless chicken thighs, cut into 1in (2½cm) pieces

2 large onions, thinly sliced

2 garlic cloves, crushed

1 tbsp ground coriander

1 tbsp ground cumin

1 tsp ground turmeric

1 tsp chili powder

1 tsp ground cardamom

½ tsp ground ginger

⅔ cup low-fat plain yogurt

1 tbsp cornstarch

1¼ cups chicken stock

⅔ cup heavy cream

1 tbsp fresh lemon juice

METHOD

1 Heat 2 tablespoons of the oil in a large frying pan over medium-high heat. In batches, add the chicken and cook, stirring occasionally, for about 5 minutes, until browned. Transfer to a plate.

2 Add the remaining 2 tablespoons of oil to the pan and reduce the heat to medium. Add the onions and garlic and cook, stirring often, about 5 minutes, until golden. Add the coriander, cumin, turmeric, chili powder, cardamom, and ginger and reduce the heat to low. Cook, stirring often, about 2 minutes, or until the spices are fragrant.

3 Mix the yogurt and cornstarch together, then stir into the pan. Stir in the remaining stock. Bring to a boil, stirring constantly. Return the chicken to the pan and simmer, stirring occasionally, for 15 minutes, or until the chicken is opaque.

4 Stir in the cream and lemon juice and simmer for 5 minutes more. Serve hot.

FREEZING INSTRUCTIONS Let stand to cool completely, then transfer to a sealable freezerproof container, making sure the chicken is well covered by the sauce. Freeze for up to 1 month. To serve, defrost in the refrigerator overnight, then reheat gently in a pan until piping hot.

GOOD WITH Herb-flecked boiled rice, naan bread, and a variety of chutneys.

serves 4

prep 20 mins
• cook 45 mins

Baked chicken with onion, garlic, and tomatoes

Simple ingredients are slow-cooked to make this a dish to savor.

INGREDIENTS

8 chicken pieces, skin on,
  about 1¾lb (800g) total
sea salt and freshly ground
  black pepper
1 tbsp all-purpose flour
2 tbsp olive oil
6 bacon slices, chopped
1 onion, finely chopped

2 garlic cloves, finely chopped
3 celery stalks, finely chopped
3 carrots, finely chopped
½ cup dry white wine
1 x 14oz (400g) can diced tomatoes,
  with juices
1¼ cups hot vegetable
  or chicken stock

METHOD

1 Preheat the oven to 400°F (200°C). Season the chicken well with salt and pepper, then dust with the flour.

2 Heat 1 tablespoon of the oil in a large cast iron or other flameproof casserole over high heat. Add the chicken pieces, skin-side down, along with the bacon, and cook the chicken for 10–15 minutes, turning once, until golden. Remove the chicken and bacon from the pan with a slotted spoon, and set aside.

3 Reduce the heat to low, and add the remaining oil to the casserole with the onion and a pinch of salt. Cook for 5 minutes until soft, then add the garlic, celery, and carrots. Cook for 5–6 minutes longer, until soft.

4 Increase the heat to high once again and add the wine. Let bubble for a few minutes until the smell of alcohol evaporates. Add the tomatoes and their juices and pour in the stock. Boil gently for a few minutes more, stirring frequently. Reduce the heat to a simmer, and return the chicken and bacon to the casserole. Spoon the tomato sauce over the chicken, cover, and transfer to the oven to cook for about 1 hour. Add more stock or hot water if it appears dry.

FREEZING INSTRUCTIONS Let stand to cool, then transfer to a sealable freezerproof container, making sure the chicken is completely covered by the sauce. Freeze for up to 3 months. To serve, defrost overnight in the refrigerator, then transfer to a casserole dish, cover, and reheat in an oven preheated to 350°F (180°C) for 30–40 minutes, or until piping hot. Add a little hot water or hot stock if the casserole starts to dry out.

GOOD WITH Creamy mashed potatoes.

serves 4

prep 5 mins
• cook 1 hr
30 mins

flameproof
casserole

Chicken and cornmeal cobbler

Using minimal fat, this dish is a healthy and tasty option.

INGREDIENTS

2 tbsp olive oil

6 skinless, boneless chicken breasts, cut into bite-sized pieces

salt and freshly ground black pepper

2 red onions, finely sliced

4 celery stalks, roughly chopped

1½ cups red wine

5 carrots, roughly chopped

3 cups hot vegetable stock

5½oz (150g) all-purpose flour, plus a little extra to dust

5½oz (150g) cornmeal

1¾oz (50g) butter

handful of fresh flat-leaf parsley, finely chopped

splash of milk

1 egg yolk, lightly beaten

METHOD

1 Heat half the oil in a large shallow cast-iron pan or flameproof casserole, season the chicken with salt and pepper, then cook over medium heat, turning occasionally for 10 minutes, or until lightly golden all over. Remove with a slotted spoon and set aside.

2 Preheat the oven to 350°F (180°C). Heat the remaining oil in the pan, then add the onions and cook over low heat for 6–8 minutes, until soft. Add the celery and cook for about 5 minutes, or until soft. Add the wine, raise the heat, and allow to boil for a couple of minutes while the alcohol evaporates. Add the carrots, return the chicken to the pan, then season well with salt and pepper. Pour in the stock and cook, uncovered, over a low heat, stirring occasionally, for 1 hour, or until all the ingredients are tender. Add a little hot water if it begins to look dry.

3 Meanwhile, put the flour, cornmeal, and a pinch of salt into a large mixing bowl. Add the butter and rub it in with your fingertips until you have a bread crumb texture. Stir through parsley, then add the milk a little at a time until the dough comes together. Form into a ball and put in the refrigerator to chill for 20 minutes. Flatten the chilled dough out on a floured surface, then roll it out with a rolling pin. Cut out about 18 rounds using the cutter, then add them to the casserole, brushing with the egg yolk before you move the pot into the oven to cook for 30 minutes more.

FREEZING INSTRUCTIONS Let stand to cool completely, then transfer to a sealable freezerproof container, making sure the meat is completely covered by sauce. Freeze for up to 3 months. To serve, defrost overnight in the refrigerator, then transfer to a casserole dish, loosely cover with foil, and reheat in an oven preheated to 350°F (180°C). Cook for 30–40 minutes, or until piping hot, adding a little hot stock if it starts to dry out. Remove the foil for the last 10 minutes of reheating.

serves 8

prep 20 mins • cook 1 hr 45 mins

healthy option

large flameproof casserole • 1½in (4cm) cutter

Chicken jalfrezi

A spicy chicken curry made with chiles and mustard seeds.

INGREDIENTS

2 tbsp vegetable oil

2 tbsp garam masala

2 tsp ground cumin

2 tsp yellow mustard seeds

1 tsp ground turmeric

salt

1 onion, sliced

1in (2.5cm) piece of fresh ginger, peeled and finely minced

3 garlic cloves, minced

1 red bell pepper, seeded and sliced

$1/2$ green bell pepper, seeded and sliced

2 fresh hot green chiles, seeded and finely minced

$1^{1}/_{2}$lb (675g) skinless, boneless chicken thighs or breasts,
    cut into 1in (2.5cm) pieces

1 cup canned chopped tomatoes

3 tbsp chopped cilantro

METHOD

1 Heat the oil in a large saucepan over medium heat. Add the garam masala, cumin, mustard seeds, and turmeric, and season with salt. Stir for 1 minute, until fragrant.

2 Add the onion, ginger, and garlic, and cook, stirring often, for about 2 minutes, until the onion starts to soften. Add the red and green peppers and the chiles and cook for 5 minutes, stirring often.

3 Increase the heat to medium-high. Add the chicken, and cook until it begins to brown. Add the tomatoes and cilantro, lower the heat, and simmer for 10 minutes, or until the chicken is cooked through, stirring frequently. Taste and season again if needed. Serve hot.

FREEZING INSTRUCTIONS Let stand to cool completely, then transfer to a sealable freezerproof container, making sure the meat is covered by sauce. Freeze for up to 3 months. To serve, defrost overnight in the refrigerator, then reheat gently in a pan, adding a little water if needed. Simmer for 15–20 minutes, or until piping hot. Alternatively, reheat in a microwave on high for 2–4 minutes, stir, and heat for 2–4 minutes more, or until piping hot. Let stand for 5 minutes before serving.

GOOD WITH Basmati rice and poppadums.

serves 4

prep 20 mins
• cook 25 mins

healthy option

Garlic and chile chicken with honey sweet potato

A sweet, comforting dish with a pleasant heat.

INGREDIENTS

8 chicken pieces (preferably a mixture of free-range thighs and drumsticks)
sea salt and freshly ground black pepper
4 sweet potatoes, peeled and coarsely chopped
1–2 tbsp honey
2 tbsp olive oil
2 fresh red jalapeño chile peppers, seeded and sliced
a few sprigs of fresh thyme
$\frac{1}{2}$ garlic bulb, cloves separated, peeled, and smashed
$\frac{1}{2}$ cup dry white wine
$1\frac{1}{4}$ cups hot chicken stock

METHOD

1 Preheat the oven to 400°F (200°C). Season the chicken well with salt and pepper and coat the sweet potatoes with the honey.

2 In a large heavy flameproof casserole, heat 1 tablespoon of the oil over medium heat. Add the sweet potatoes and cook for 5 minutes until beginning to brown, then remove from the pan and set aside.

3 Increase the heat to medium-high, and heat the remaining oil in the same pan. Brown the chicken for about 5 minutes on each side until nicely golden all over. Add the chiles, thyme, and garlic. Return the sweet potatoes to the pan, and season well.

4 Pour in the wine and stock, cover the pan, and transfer to the oven to cook for 1 hour. Check the casserole a few times during cooking, stirring if needed, and add a small amount of stock if it is too dry.

FREEZING INSTRUCTIONS Let stand to cool, then transfer to sealable freezerproof containers, making sure the chicken is completely covered by sauce (add a little more cold stock if it isn't). Freeze for up to 3 months. To serve, defrost overnight in the refrigerator, then transfer to a casserole dish, and add a little hot stock. Cover, and reheat in an oven preheated to 350°F (180°C) for 30–40 minutes, or until piping hot. Add more hot stock if it starts to dry out.

GOOD WITH Thick slices of fresh crusty bread.

serves 4

prep 15 mins
• cook 1 hr
10 mins

healthy option

flameproof
casserole

Beef shank with Marsala

Marsala is a fortified wine from Sicily that is popular in Italian cooking. French lentils add extra body and flavor to this hearty casserole.

INGREDIENTS
$3\frac{1}{2}$lb (1.6kg) beef shank, cut into bite-sized pieces
all-purpose flour, to dust
sea salt and freshly ground black pepper
3 tbsp olive oil
2 red onions, roughly chopped
4 carrots, roughly chopped
$1\frac{1}{4}$ cups Marsala
7oz (200g) French lentils, rinsed and picked over
5 cups hot vegetable stock
2 bay leaves

METHOD
1 Preheat the oven to 350°F (180°C). Dust the meat with a little flour, then season with salt and pepper. Heat half the oil in a large cast-iron casserole, add the meat, and cook over medium heat, stirring often, for 10 minutes, or until browned on all sides. Remove with a slotted spoon and set aside.

2 Heat the remaining oil in the casserole, add the onions, and cook over low heat for 6–8 minutes, or until soft. Stir in the carrots and cook for 5 minutes. Return the meat to the pan, pour in the Marsala, and let it bubble for a few minutes while the alcohol evaporates. Stir in the lentils, add the stock, and bring to a boil. Season with salt and pepper, then add the bay leaves. Cover and put in the oven to cook for $1\frac{1}{2}$ hours. Check occasionally and add a little hot water if it looks dry. Serve hot.

FREEZING INSTRUCTIONS Let stand to cool completely, then transfer to a sealable freezerproof container, making sure the meat is covered by sauce. Freeze for up to 3 months. To serve, defrost overnight in the refrigerator, then reheat gently in a pan, adding a little hot water if the sauce is too thick. Simmer for 15–20 minutes, or until piping hot. Alternatively, reheat in a microwave on high for 3–4 minutes, stir, and heat for 3–4 minutes more, or until piping hot. Let stand for 5 minutes before serving.

GOOD WITH Fresh crusty bread.

serves 8

prep 25 mins
• cook 1 hr
30 mins

large
flameproof
casserole

Pork with fennel and mustard

If speed is what you need, this lively dish is the perfect quick fix.

INGREDIENTS

6 tbsp olive oil
2 large onions, sliced
3 fennel bulbs, sliced
2½lb (1.1kg) lean pork, cut into ¾in (2cm) cubes
8 garlic cloves, chopped
⅔ cup dry white wine
2 tbsp whole- or coarse-grain mustard
1 tsp paprika
large handful of flat-leaf parsley, coarsely chopped
1 tbsp chopped fresh sage leaves
1 tbsp chopped fresh rosemary leaves
2 tbsp all-purpose flour
3 cups milk
sea salt and freshly ground black pepper

METHOD

1 Heat the oil in a large heavy-based pot, add the onions and fennel, and cook for 5 minutes, or until beginning to soften. Add the pork and cook, stirring occasionally, for 5 minutes, or until no longer pink. Add the garlic and cook for 1 minute, then stir in the wine and mustard, raise the heat, and allow to bubble for 3 minutes while the alcohol evaporates.

2 Stir in the paprika, parsley, sage, and rosemary, then add the flour and mix well. Add a little of the milk, mix to an even paste, then stir in the rest of it. Season with salt and pepper and cook for 5 minutes, adding a little more milk if it looks dry.

FREEZING INSTRUCTIONS Let stand to cool, then transfer to a sealable freezerproof container, making sure the pork is completely covered by the sauce. Freeze for up to 3 months. To serve, defrost overnight in the refrigerator, then transfer to a casserole dish, add a little hot stock, and cover. Reheat in an oven preheated to 350°F (180°C) for 25 minutes, or until piping hot. Add a little more stock if it starts to dry out.

GOOD WITH Mashed new potatoes or creamy mashed potatoes.

serves 8

prep 20 mins
• cook 20 mins

Pork goulash

This thick stew from Hungary is distinctive for its flavors of paprika, caraway seeds, garlic, and onion. It can also be made with beef.

INGREDIENTS

2½lb (1.1kg) pork shoulder, cut into bite-sized pieces
1 tbsp all-purpose flour
2 tsp paprika
2 tsp caraway seeds, crushed
sea salt and freshly ground black pepper
2 tbsp olive oil
1 tbsp cider vinegar
2 tbsp tomato paste or purée
4 cups hot vegetable stock
6 tomatoes, skinned and roughly chopped
1 onion, sliced into rings, to serve
handful of curly parsley, finely chopped, to serve

METHOD

1 Toss the meat with the flour, paprika, and caraway seeds, and season with salt and pepper. Heat the oil in a large cast-iron casserole, then add the meat and cook over high heat, stirring occasionally, for 8–10 minutes, or until the pork begins to brown. Add the vinegar and stir for a couple of minutes, scraping up any brown bits that are stuck to the bottom of the pan.

2 Add the tomato paste, followed by the stock, and bring to a boil. Reduce to a simmer, cover, and cook over low heat for 1 hour. Check occasionally and add a little boiling water if the goulash begins to dry out too much—it should remain fairly thick, though.

3 Stir in the tomatoes, season to taste if needed, then top with the onion rings and parsley and serve.

FREEZING INSTRUCTIONS Let stand to cool, then transfer to a sealable freezerproof container, making sure the pork and tomatoes are completely covered by the sauce. Freeze for up to 3 months. To serve, defrost overnight in the refrigerator, then reheat in a pan, adding a little hot water or hot stock. Simmer for 15–20 minutes, or until piping hot. Add some onion rings and chopped parsley to serve.

GOOD WITH Steamed rice.

serves 8

prep 25 mins
• cook 1 hr

large
cast-iron pan

Lamb daube

One of the great Provençal dishes, daubes feature marinated meat that is braised slowly in wine. Orange zest, star anise, and olives are typical ingredients.

INGREDIENTS

3lb (1.35kg) lamb shoulder or leg of lamb, cut into bite-sized pieces

1¼ cups red wine

1 star anise

zest of 1 orange, grated

sea salt and freshly ground black pepper

3 tbsp olive oil

2 onions, finely chopped

14oz (400g) bacon or pancetta, cut into bite-sized pieces

4 celery stalks, finely chopped

4 carrots, finely chopped

4 leeks, cleaned and coarsely chopped

4 cups hot vegetable stock

2 handfuls of pitted green olives

METHOD

1 Put the lamb, wine, star anise, and orange zest in a bowl, season with salt and pepper, cover, and marinate for 30 minutes (or overnight in the fridge).

2 Preheat the oven to 400°F (200°C). Heat half the oil in a large cast-iron pot. Remove the meat with a slotted spoon (reserve the marinade) and add to the pot. Cook over medium heat, stirring often, for 10 minutes, or until browned all over. Remove with a slotted spoon and set aside. Heat the remaining oil in the pot, add the onions, and cook over low heat for 6–8 minutes, or until soft. Stir in the bacon or pancetta and cook for 6–10 minutes, or until crispy. Add the celery and carrots and cook over low heat, adding more oil if needed, for 5 minutes, or until they begin to soften.

3 Stir in the leeks and cook for a few minutes, then return the meat to the pot and pour in the marinade and stock. Stir in the olives, bring to a boil, then season with salt and pepper. Cover with a lid and cook in the oven for 30 minutes. Turn the oven down to 300°F (150°C) and cook for another 1½–2 hours. Check occasionally and add a little hot water if the daube looks dry. Serve hot.

FREEZING INSTRUCTIONS Let stand to cool completely, then transfer to a sealable freezerproof container, making sure the meat is well covered by the sauce. Freeze for up to 3 months. To serve, defrost overnight in the refrigerator, then reheat gently in a pan for 15–20 minutes, or until piping hot. Alternatively, place in a casserole dish, cover, and reheat in an oven preheated to 350°F (180°C) for 30–40 minutes, or until piping hot. Add a little hot stock if it starts to dry out.

GOOD WITH Sautéed potatoes and crusty bread.

serves 8

prep 25 mins, plus marinating • cook 2 hrs 30 mins

healthy option

large flameproof casserole

Pork with rice and tomatoes

Big, bold, and filling—this makes a super family meal.

INGREDIENTS

6 tbsp olive oil
3 onions, diced
2$\frac{1}{2}$lb (1.1kg) lean pork, cut into
   2in (5cm) chunks
6 garlic cloves, finely chopped
handful of flat-leaf parsley, chopped
1 tbsp fresh thyme
1 tbsp chopped fresh sage leaves
2 tsp paprika
$\frac{2}{3}$ cup dry white wine
1$\frac{1}{4}$lb (550g) long-grain rice
2 x 28oz (800g) cans diced tomatoes
sea salt and freshly ground black pepper

METHOD

1 Preheat the oven to 300°F (150°C). Heat the oil in a large, heavy-based, oven-safe pot, add the onions, and cook over medium heat for 5 minutes, or until they start to soften. Add the pork and cook for 5 minutes, or until no longer pink. Stir in the garlic, parsley, thyme, sage, and paprika, then add the wine and cook for 5 minutes. Add the rice and tomatoes, stir to combine, then season well with salt and pepper.

2 Cover and cook in the oven for 1 hour. Stir occasionally and add a little hot water if it starts to dry out. Remove from the oven and let stand for 10 minutes with the lid on before serving.

FREEZING INSTRUCTIONS Let stand to cool completely, then transfer to sealable freezerproof containers, making sure the pork is well covered. Freeze for up to 1 month. To serve, defrost in the refrigerator overnight, then reheat in a microwave on high for 3–4 minutes, stir then heat for 3–4 minutes more, or until piping hot. Let stand for 5 minutes before serving.

serves 6–8

prep 30 mins
• cook 1 hr

Sauerbraten

Wonderfully tender German-style beef with a richly spiced sauce.

INGREDIENTS
2¼lb (1kg) beef chuck
    or round roast
2 tbsp vegetable oil
1 onion, sliced
1 celery stalk, chopped
1 tbsp all-purpose flour
⅓ cup crushed gingersnap cookies
salt and freshly ground black pepper

For the marinade
2 cups hearty red wine
⅔ cup red wine vinegar
2 onions, thinly sliced
1 tbsp light brown sugar
½ tsp freshly grated nutmeg
4 whole allspice berries, lightly crushed
4 black peppercorns, lightly crushed
2 bay leaves, crumbled
½ tsp salt

METHOD

1 Bring the wine, vinegar, ⅔ cup water, onions, sugar, nutmeg, allspice, peppercorns, bay leaves, and salt to a boil in a saucepan. Let cool completely.

2 Place the beef in a bowl and pour in the cooled marinade. Cover with plastic wrap and refrigerate, turning the meat over every 8 hours or so, for 2–3 days.

3 Preheat the oven to 350°F (180°C). Lift the beef from the marinade, drain well, then pat dry with paper towels. Strain the marinade into a bowl, discarding the spices.

4 Heat the oil in a large flameproof casserole over medium-high heat. Add the beef and cook about 10 minutes, until browned on all sides. Transfer to a plate. Add the onion and celery to the casserole and cook, stirring constantly, for about 5 minutes, until beginning to brown. Sprinkle in the flour and stir for 1 minute. Stir in 2 cups of the reserved marinade and bring to a boil, stirring often.

5 Return the beef to the casserole and baste with the liquid. Cover tightly. Bake for about 2¼ hours, or until very tender.

6 Transfer the beef to a serving platter and tent with aluminum foil. Strain the cooking liquid into another saucepan, bring to a boil, and cook until reduced to about 1¼ cups. Whisk in the gingersnap cookie crumbs and cook, whisking often, until the sauce is smooth and lightly thickened. Season with salt and pepper. Slice the beef crosswise, spread the slices on the platter, and spoon some of the sauce over. Serve hot, with the rest of the sauce on the side.

FREEZING INSTRUCTIONS Let stand to cool, then transfer to a sealable freezerproof container, making sure the meat is well covered by the sauce. Freeze for up to 2 months. To serve, defrost in the refrigerator overnight, then cover with plastic wrap and reheat in a microwave on high for 3–4 minutes. Stir, and heat for 3–4 minutes more, or until piping hot.

GOOD WITH Potato dumplings and green vegetables.

serves 4–6

prep 30 mins,
plus marinating
• cook 2–2¼ hrs

marinate for
2–3 days

large flameproof
casserole

Beef and celery root casserole with stout and anchovies

A rich casserole with earthy flavors.

INGREDIENTS
3 tbsp olive oil
2½lb (1.1kg) beef stew meat or pot roast, cut into
   bite-sized pieces
2 onions, finely chopped
handful of fresh thyme leaves
8 salted anchovies
1 large celery root, peeled and cut into bite-sized pieces
2 cups bottle stout
4 cups hot vegetable stock
sea salt and freshly ground black pepper
5 medium potatoes, cut into chunky pieces

METHOD
1 Preheat the oven to 350°F (180°C). Heat half the oil in a large cast-iron pot, add the meat, and cook over medium heat, stirring occasionally, for 10 minutes, or until evenly browned. Remove with a slotted spoon and set aside. Heat the remaining oil in the pan, add the onions and thyme, and cook over low heat for 6–8 minutes, or until soft.

2 Stir in the anchovies, then stir in the celery root and cook for 5–8 minutes. Add a little of the stout and stir to scrape up any bits that are stuck to the bottom of the pan. Add the remaining stout and the stock, season with salt and pepper, then return the meat to the pot, cover with a lid, and put in the oven for 1 hour.

3 Add the potatoes with a little hot water if the casserole looks dry. Cook for 30 minutes, or until the potatoes are cooked and the beef is tender.

FREEZING INSTRUCTIONS Let stand to cool completely, then transfer to a sealable freezerproof container, making sure the meat is well covered by the sauce. Freeze for up to 3 months. To serve, defrost in the refrigerator overnight, then reheat in a pan. Simmer gently for 15–20 minutes, adding hot water or hot stock if needed, until piping hot. Alternatively, put in a casserole dish, cover, and reheat in an oven preheated to 350°F (180°C) for 30–40 minutes, or until piping hot.

GOOD WITH Mashed potatoes and steamed cabbage.

serves 8

**prep 30 mins
• cook 1 hr
30 mins**

**large
flameproof
casserole**

Pork and bean casserole

Using canned beans instead of dried ones makes this satisfying casserole quite quick to prepare.

INGREDIENTS

6 tbsp olive oil
3 large onions, diced
6 celery stalks, diced
$2^{1}/_{2}$lb (1.1kg) lean pork, cut into $^{3}/_{4}$in (2cm) cubes
2 tsp paprika
1 x 14oz (400g) can cannellini beans, drained and rinsed
1 x 14oz (400g) can flageolet beans, drained and rinsed
1 x 14oz (400g) can lima beans, drained and rinsed
8 garlic cloves, finely chopped
$^{2}/_{3}$ cup dry white wine
$1^{1}/_{4}$ cups hot vegetable stock
juice of 1 lemon
handful of fresh flat-leaf parsley, chopped
sea salt and freshly ground black pepper

METHOD

1 Heat the oil in a large heavy-based pot over medium heat, add the onions and celery, and cook, stirring, for 5 minutes, or until soft. Add the pork and cook, stirring occasionally, until no longer pink. Stir in the paprika, then add the beans and garlic and cook for 1 minute.

2 Stir in the wine and let bubble for 3 minutes while the alcohol evaporates. Add the stock, lemon juice, and parsley, and season with salt and pepper. Bring to a boil, then lower the heat and simmer for 20 minutes.

FREEZING INSTRUCTIONS Let stand to cool, then transfer to a sealable freezerproof container, making sure the pork is completely covered by the sauce. Freeze for up to 3 months. To serve, defrost overnight in the refrigerator, then reheat gently in a pan for 15–20 minutes, or until piping hot. Add a little hot water or hot stock if it gets too dry. Alternatively, reheat in a microwave for 2–3 minutes on high, then stir and heat for 2–3 minutes more, or until piping hot.

GOOD WITH Steamed rice.

serves 8

prep 20 mins
• cook 20 mins

healthy option

Lamb braised with green peas and preserved lemons

The fresh, herby flavors of this Morrocan-inspired dish are appealing in summer.

INGREDIENTS

2 onions, finely chopped
3 tbsp chopped parsley, plus more for garnish
3 tbsp chopped cilantro, plus more for garnish
3 garlic cloves, chopped
1 tsp peeled and grated fresh ginger
$1/2$ cup olive oil
$2^1/_4$lb (1kg) boneless leg of lamb, cut into thick slices
$2^1/_4$ cups lamb or beef stock
2 preserved lemons (available at specialty grocers)
salt and freshly ground black pepper
1lb (450g) frozen peas
lemon zest, to garnish

METHOD

1 Combine the onions, parsley, cilantro, garlic, ginger, and olive oil in a large dish. Add the lamb. Cover and refrigerate for at least 8 hours.

2 Remove the lamb, reserving the marinade. Heat a frying pan over medium-high heat. In batches, add the lamb and cook, turning occasionally, about 5 minutes, until browned. Transfer the lamb to a flameproof casserole.

3 Add the marinade and stock to the casserole and bring to a boil over high heat. Reduce the heat to medium-low and cover. Simmer for 1 hour.

4 Cut the preserved lemons into quarters, discard the flesh, then thinly slice the rinds. Add to the pan and continue simmering for another 30 minutes, or until the lamb is very tender.

5 Season with salt and pepper. Stir in the peas and simmer about 5 minutes, until they are cooked. Sprinkle with lots of chopped parsley and cilantro and serve hot, with lemon zest.

FREEZING INSTRUCTIONS Let stand to cool, then transfer to sealable freezerproof containers, making sure the lamb is completely covered by the sauce (add a little more cold stock if it isn't). Freeze for up to 3 months. To serve, defrost overnight in the refrigerator, then transfer to a casserole dish, and add a little hot stock. Cover, and reheat in an oven preheated to 350°F (180°C) for 30–40 minutes, or until piping hot. Add more hot stock if it starts to dry out. Serve with chopped parsley and cilantro and lemon zest.

GOOD WITH Couscous or rice.

serves 6

prep 15 mins,
plus marinating
• cook 1 hr
40 mins

marinate
overnight

large flameproof
casserole

Chili con carne

A really good chili con carne recipe is a great staple for any kitchen.

INGREDIENTS
6 tbsp olive oil
3 large onions, diced
$2^1/_2$lb (1.1kg) lean ground beef
$^2/_3$ cup dry sherry
8 garlic cloves, chopped
4 green bird's-eye chiles, finely chopped
1 tsp cayenne pepper
1 tsp paprika
2 x 14oz (400g) cans kidney beans, drained and rinsed
4 bay leaves
3 x 14oz (400g) cans chopped tomatoes
2 tsp dried oregano
sea salt and freshly ground black pepper

METHOD
1 Heat the oil in a large heavy-based pan, add the onions, and cook, for 5 minutes, or until starting to soften. Add the meat and cook over medium heat, stirring, until no longer pink. Stir in the sherry and garlic and cook for 1 minute, then add the chiles, cayenne, and paprika and cook for 5 minutes.

2 Add the kidney beans and bay leaves, cook for 2 minutes, then add the tomatoes and oregano. Bring to a boil, season, then simmer over low heat for 40 minutes, stirring occasionally. Season with salt and pepper. Serve hot.

FREEZING INSTRUCTIONS Let stand to cool, then transfer to sealable freezerproof containers. Freeze for up to 3 months. To serve, defrost overnight in the refrigerator, then reheat in a pan, adding a little water to prevent scorching. Simmer for 15–20 minutes, stirring frequently, until piping hot. Alternatively, reheat in a microwave on high for 2–3 minutes, then stir and heat for 2–3 minutes more, or until piping hot. Let stand for 5 minutes before serving.

GOOD WITH Steamed or boiled rice.

serves 8

prep 30 mins
• cook 40 mins

healthy option

94

Spiced sausage cassoulet

A generous pinch of paprika lifts this classic French sausage-and-bean dish.

INGREDIENTS

4 tbsp olive oil
2 large onions, sliced
4 celery stalks, chopped
2 large potatoes, cut into ³/₄in
   (2cm) cubes
16 sweet pork sausages
7oz (200g) slab bacon, cut into thin
   strips or lardons
6 garlic cloves, chopped
2 x 14oz (400g) cans navy beans,
   drained and rinsed

1 tbsp tomato paste or purée
3 tsp paprika
2 tsp dried thyme
2 tsp dried oregano
1 tsp freshly ground black pepper
1¹/₄ cups dry white wine
2 cups hot vegetable stock
4¹/₂oz (125g) fresh bread crumbs
handful flat-leaf parsley, chopped
3 tbsp butter

METHOD

1 Preheat the oven to 300°F (150°C). Heat the oil in a large heavy-based casserole, add the onions, celery, and potatoes, and cook for 5 minutes, or until starting to soften. Add the sausages and bacon and cook for 5 minutes, until starting to brown.

2 Add the garlic and cook for 1 minute, then add the navy beans, tomato paste, paprika, thyme, oregano, and pepper. Combine well, then add the wine. Bring to a boil and simmer for 2 minutes, then add the stock and 1¹/₄ cups hot water. Bring to a boil, simmer for 10 minutes, then remove from heat.

3 Mix the bread crumbs with the parsley and cover the top of the dish liberally. Dot with pats of butter, cover, and bake for 1¹/₂ hours. Uncover and cook for another 30 minutes. Serve hot.

FREEZING INSTRUCTIONS Let stand to cool completely, then transfer to a sealable freezerproof container, making sure the sausages are completely covered by the sauce. Freeze for up to 3 months. To serve, defrost in the refrigerator overnight, then cover loosely with plastic wrap and reheat in a microwave on high for 2–3 minutes. Agitate, and heat for 2–3 minutes more, or until piping hot. Let stand for 5 minutes before serving.

GOOD WITH Crisp green salad.

serves 8

prep 30 mins
• cook 2 hrs

Beef stew with orange and bay leaves

This attractive stew, which has a light sauce, is spiced with cinnamon and nutmeg to complement the flavor of the oranges.

INGREDIENTS

3 tbsp olive oil
3lb (1.35kg) beef stew meat, cut into bite-sized pieces
sea salt and freshly ground black pepper
$1\frac{1}{2}$ cups dry white wine
3 bay leaves
6 cups hot vegetable stock
2 cinnamon sticks
2 x 14oz (400g) cans chickpeas, drained, rinsed, and drained again
2 oranges, peeled and sliced into rings
handful of fresh cilantro, finely chopped, to serve

METHOD

1 Preheat the oven to 350°F (180°C). Heat the oil in a large cast-iron casserole, add the meat, season with salt and pepper, and cook over medium heat, stirring occasionally, for 10 minutes, or until brown on all sides. Carefully add the wine (it will spit) then stir the meat around the pan and allow the liquid to bubble for a couple of minutes while the alcohol evaporates.

2 Add the bay leaves, then pour in the stock. Add the cinnamon and nutmeg and season again with salt and pepper. Bring to a boil, add the chickpeas, then cover with a lid and put in the oven to cook for 1 hour. Add the oranges and cook for 30 minutes. Stir in the cilantro and serve.

FREEZING INSTRUCTIONS Let stand to cool completely, then transfer to a sealable freezerproof container, making sure the meat is well covered by the sauce. Freeze for up to 3 months. To serve, defrost overnight in the refrigerator, then reheat in a pan, adding a little hot water or hot stock. Simmer gently for 15 minutes, or until piping hot. Stir in some chopped cilantro to serve.

GOOD WITH Fresh crusty bread.

serves 8

prep 30 mins
• cook 1 hr
30 mins

large
flameproof
casserole

Sausages with lima beans

This satisfying dinner dish is especially good on a cold winter evening.

INGREDIENTS

12 sweet Italian pork sausages
1 tbsp olive oil
1 onion, sliced
1 celery stalk, chopped
2 garlic cloves, crushed
$^1/_3$ cup white wine
1 x 14.5oz (411g) can chopped tomatoes
3 tbsp ketchup
1 tsp sweet paprika
salt and freshly ground black pepper
$1^1/_2$ cups thawed frozen lima beans
1 tbsp chopped basil or parsley

METHOD

1 Position a broiler rack 6in (15cm) from the source of heat and preheat the broiler. Prick the sausages with a fork. Arrange on the broiler rack and broil about 10 minutes, turning occasionally, until cooked through. Transfer to a plate.

2 Meanwhile, heat the oil in a saucepan over medium-low heat. Add the onion, celery, and garlic, and cook, stirring frequently, about 5 minutes, or until softened. Increase the heat to medium-high and add the wine. Bring to a boil, then stir in the canned tomatoes with their juices. Stir in the ketchup and paprika, season with salt and pepper, and bring to a boil. Reduce the heat to medium-low and simmer, uncovered, for about 20 minutes, or until slightly thickened.

3 Stir in the lima beans and sausages. Simmer for 10 minutes. Sprinkle with basil or parsley and serve hot.

FREEZING INSTRUCTIONS Let stand to cool completely, then transfer to a sealable freezerproof container, making sure the sausages are completely covered by the sauce. Freeze for up to 3 months. To serve, defrost in the refrigerator overnight, then cover loosely with plastic wrap and reheat in a microwave on high for 3–4 minutes. Agitate, and heat for 3–4 minutes more, or until piping hot. Let stand for 5 minutes. Serve with a sprinkling of chopped fresh herbs.

GOOD WITH Creamy mashed potatoes or a carrot-and-potato mash.

serves 4

prep 10 mins
• cook 30 mins

Lamb, spinach, and chickpea hotpot

Hectic weeknights call for easy, wholesome dishes such as this one.

INGREDIENTS

1¹/₂lb (675g) lean lamb, cut into ³/₄in (2cm) cubes
2 tbsp all-purpose flour
1 tsp paprika
6 tbsp olive oil
2 large red onions, diced
6 garlic cloves, chopped
2 x 14oz (400g) cans chickpeas, drained and rinsed
³/₄ cup dry white wine
2 x 14oz (400g) cans diced tomatoes
sea salt and freshly ground black pepper
1¹/₄lb (550g) baby leaf spinach

METHOD

1 Put the lamb, flour, and paprika in a mixing bowl and combine well. Heat the oil in a large heavy-based pot over medium heat, add the onions, and cook, stirring frequently, for 5 minutes, or until soft. Add the lamb and cook, stirring occasionally, for 5 minutes, or until evenly browned. Stir in the garlic and chickpeas and cook for 1 minute.

2 Pour in the wine and simmer for about 3 minutes, while the alcohol evaporates. Add the tomatoes, bring to a boil, reduce the heat, and simmer for 15 minutes. Season with salt and pepper, stir in the spinach, and cook for 3 minutes. Serve hot.

FREEZING INSTRUCTIONS Let stand to cool completely, then transfer to a sealable freezerproof container, making sure the meat is completely covered by the sauce. Freeze for up to 3 months. To serve, defrost overnight in the refrigerator, then transfer to a deep ovenproof dish, cover, and reheat in an oven preheated to 350°F (180°C) for 15–20 minutes, or until piping hot. Add a little hot water or hot stock if it starts to dry out. Alternatively, microwave on high for 3–4 minutes, stir, then heat for 3–4 minutes more, or until piping hot. Let stand for 5 minutes before serving.

GOOD WITH Steamed or boiled rice.

serves 8

prep 25 mins
• cook 30 mins

healthy option

Game stew

Packs of mixed game can be bought ready-diced, cutting down on preparation time and producing a richly flavored stew.

INGREDIENTS

3lb (1.35kg) (boned weight) mixed game, such as pheasant, venison, and duck, cut into bite-sized pieces
all-purpose flour, to dust
sea salt and freshly ground black pepper
2 tbsp olive oil
2 tbsp brandy
2 onions, finely chopped

4 garlic cloves, finely chopped
4 celery stalks, finely diced
4 carrots, finely diced
1 bouquet garni
1¼lb (550g) cremini mushrooms, quartered
1½ cups dry white wine
1 tbsp red currant jelly
5 cups hot chicken stock

METHOD

1 Preheat the oven to 350°F (180°C). Dust the meat lightly with flour, then season. Heat half the oil in a large cast-iron pot, add the meat, and cook over medium heat, stirring, for 6–8 minutes, or until browned on all sides. Remove with a slotted spoon and set aside.

2 Add the brandy to the pot and stir to deglaze, add the rest of the oil and onions and cook over low heat for 6 minutes, or until soft. Stir in the garlic, celery, carrots, and bouquet garni, and cook over low heat, stirring often, for 8 minutes, or until tender.

3 Stir in the mushrooms, raise the heat, add the wine, and allow to bubble for 2 minutes while the alcohol evaporates. Stir in the red currant jelly, then pour in the stock. Cover with a lid and put in the oven for 1 hour, or until the meat is tender.

FREEZING INSTRUCTIONS Let stand to cool completely, then transfer to a sealable freezerproof container, making sure the meat is completely covered by the sauce. Freeze for up to 3 months. To serve, defrost in the refrigerator overnight, then reheat gently in a pan. Simmer for 15–20 minutes, adding hot water if it starts to dry out, until piping hot.

GOOD WITH Creamy mashed potatoes.

serves 8

prep 30 mins
• cook 1 hr

large
cast-iron pan

Swedish meatballs

Although regarded as Swedish, these are popular all over Scandinavia.

INGREDIENTS
$^1/_2$ cup fresh bread crumbs
$^1/_2$ cup heavy cream
4 tbsp butter
1 small onion, finely chopped
8oz (230g) ground sirloin
8oz (230g) ground lamb
1 large egg, beaten
$^1/_4$ tsp freshly grated nutmeg
salt and freshly ground black pepper

For the sauce
$^3/_4$ cup heavy cream
$^1/_2$ cup beef or lamb stock

METHOD
1 Combine the bread crumbs and cream in a large bowl, then set aside. Meanwhile, heat 1 tablespoon of butter in a frying pan over medium-low heat. Add the onion and cook about 4 minutes, until translucent. Let cool.

2 Add the beef, lamb, cooled onions, egg, and nutmeg to the soaked bread crumbs and season with salt and pepper. Cover with plastic wrap and refrigerate for 1 hour.

3 With damp hands, shape the meat mixture firmly into balls about the size of ping pong balls, and place on a baking sheet. Cover and refrigerate again for about 1 hour.

4 Melt the remaining 3 tablespoons of butter in a large frying pan over medium heat. In batches, add the meatballs and cook, turning occasionally, for 10 minutes, until evenly browned and cooked through. Using a slotted spoon, transfer to paper towels to drain. Transfer to a bowl and tent with aluminum foil to keep warm.

5 Pour the fat from the pan. Add the cream and stock, bring to a boil over medium heat, and cook about 2 minutes, until slightly thickened. Drizzle with meatballs with the sauce, and serve hot.

FREEZING INSTRUCTIONS Omit the sauce when freezing. Freeze the meatballs either uncooked or cooked and cooled. Transfer to a sealable freezerproof container and freeze for up to 3 months. To serve, defrost overnight in the refrigerator. If uncooked, fry as per Step 4. If cooked, reheat in a microwave on high for 2–3 minutes, agitate, and heat for 2–3 minutes more, or until piping hot. Prepare the sauce as per Step 5 and drizzle over the meatballs.

GOOD WITH New potatoes and steamed broccoli.

serves 4

prep 30 mins,
plus chilling
• cook 20 mins

Spanish meatballs

These veal and pork meatballs, *albóndigas* in Spanish, are popular as tapas.

INGREDIENTS

750g (1lb 10oz) minced veal
250g (9oz) minced pork
2 garlic cloves, grated or finely chopped
115g (4oz) flat-leaf parsley, finely chopped
salt and freshly ground black pepper
$\frac{1}{2}$ tsp ground nutmeg
5 tbsp dry breadcrumbs
100ml ($3\frac{1}{2}$fl oz) milk

METHOD

1 Place the veal, pork, garlic, and parsley into a bowl, and mix together well. Season with pepper and nutmeg, and set aside.

2 Put the breadcrumbs in another bowl, pour in the milk, and set aside to soak.

3 Heat the olive oil in the casserole over a medium heat, and cook the onions, stirring, for 4–5 minutes, or until softened. Sprinkle in the flour and continue to cook for a further 1 minute. Pour in the wine, and season to taste with salt and pepper. Bring to a simmer, then reduce the heat and cook for 15 minutes, or until the sauce is reduced. Press the sauce through a sieve and return to the casserole, over a low heat.

4 Squeeze the excess milk from the breadcrumbs and add the crumbs to the meat with the eggs and 3 tablespoons of the reduced sauce. Mix thoroughly, then roll the mixture into golfball-sized balls, and dust each with a little flour.

5 Heat the sunflower oil in a large frying pan. Working in batches, fry the meatballs, turning frequently, for 5 minutes, or until evenly browned. Remove them from the pan, drain on kitchen paper, and transfer to the casserole.

6 Poach the meatballs gently in the sauce for 20 minutes, or until the meatballs are no longer pink when cut in half. Serve warm, with the sauce poured over, and garnished with parsley.

FREEZING INSTRUCTIONS Leave to cool completely, then transfer to a sealable freezerproof container, making sure the meatballs are covered by the sauce. Freeze for up to 3 months. To serve, defrost in the refrigerator overnight, then reheat in a microwave at High for 2–3 minutes, agitate, and heat for a further 2–3 minutes. Leave to stand for 5 minutes. Serve with a sprinkling of chopped parsley.

GOOD WITH Crusty bread or with olive herbed mashed potatoes and green beans.

makes 48

prep 20 mins
• cook 1 hr

large
flameproof
casserole

Chicken schnitzels

A quick dish that is suitable for a family supper or dinner party.

INGREDIENTS

$^1/_3$ cup all-purpose flour
1 large egg
$^1/_2$ cup fine dry bread crumbs
4 skinless, boneless chicken breasts
salt and freshly ground black pepper
6 tbsp canola oil
4 lemon halves, to serve

METHOD

1 Spread the flour in a shallow bowl, beat the egg in another bowl, and spread the bread crumbs in a third bowl.

2 Put the chicken breasts and the thin, small fillets between 2 sheets of wax paper and pound with a rolling pin until they are about $^1/_4$in (5mm) thick. Season with salt and pepper.

3 Coat the chicken one piece at a time, first in the flour, then in the beaten egg, and then in the bread crumbs, pressing them on to both sides. Refrigerate, uncovered, for at least 30 minutes. Preheat the oven to 200°F (95°C).

4 When ready to cook, heat 3 tablespoons of the oil in a very large nonstick frying pan over medium-high heat until hot. Add 2 schnitzels to the pan and fry for 3 minutes on each side, until golden brown, and the juices run clear when pierced with the tip of a knife.

5 Drain the schnitzels well on paper towels, and keep warm in the oven. Heat the remaining oil in the pan, then add the remaining schnitzels, and fry as above. Serve with the lemon halves.

FREEZING INSTRUCTIONS Let stand to cool, then freeze in a sealable freezerproof container for up to 3 months. To serve, defrost overnight in the refrigerator, then transfer to an oiled baking tray. Reheat in an oven preheated to 350°F (180°C) for 20–30 minutes, or until piping hot. Serve with lemon wedges.

GOOD WITH Sautéed potatoes and green beans.

serves 4

**prep 10 mins,
plus chilling
• cook 12 mins**

Salmon fish cakes

These fish cakes could also be made with leftover roast salmon.

INGREDIENTS

1lb (450g) baking potatoes, such as
   Russet Burbank, peeled and cubed
2lb (900g) skinless salmon fillets
1 onion, halved
a few black peppercorns
2 bay leaves
4 whole scallions, finely chopped
3 tbsp chopped dill
2 tbsp prepared horseradish
grated zest of 1 lemon

2 tbsp fresh lemon juice
pinch of cayenne
salt and freshly ground black pepper

For the coating
1$\frac{1}{2}$ cups fresh bread crumbs
4 tbsp chopped chives or parsley
$\frac{1}{2}$ cup all-purpose flour
2 large eggs, beaten
$\frac{1}{2}$ cup vegetable oil

METHOD

1 Boil the potatoes in salted water over medium heat about 20 minutes, or until very tender. Drain well, return to the pan, and mash.

2 Meanwhile, place the salmon in a frying pan and cover with cold water. Add the onion, peppercorns, and bay leaves. Bring to a boil, then simmer for 5 minutes. Remove from the heat, drain in a colander, and let cool completely, about 20 minutes.

3 Flake the salmon into a large bowl. Add the mashed potatoes, scallions, dill, horseradish, lemon zest and juice, and cayenne and mix well. Season with salt and pepper. Shape into 12 round cakes. If you have time, refrigerate 1 hour before cooking.

4 Process the bread crumbs and chives in a food processor until well combined. Put the flour, eggs, and bread crumbs in shallow dishes. Coat the salmon cakes in flour, then egg, then the herbed bread crumbs.

5 Heat the oil in a frying pan over medium heat. In batches, add the salmon cakes and cook for about 3 minutes on each side, or until crisp and golden brown. Transfer to paper towels to drain. Serve hot.

FREEZING INSTRUCTIONS Freeze the fish cakes either uncooked or cooked and cooled. Wrap each individually in wax paper then double wrap in plastic wrap, or transfer to a sealable freezerproof container, and freeze for up to 3 months. To thaw, unwrap and place on a plate, or in the container, in the refrigerator to defrost overnight. If uncooked, fry as per Step 5. If cooked, transfer to an oiled baking tray and reheat in an oven preheated to 350°F (180°C) for 20–30 minutes, or until piping hot. Serve with lemon wedges.

GOOD WITH Hot french fries, garden peas, and lemon wedges.

serves 6

prep 30 mins,
plus cooling
and chilling
• cook 30 mins

Mixed fish kebabs

Use fish with a firm texture for these tasty kebabs.

INGREDIENTS

5$\frac{1}{2}$oz (150g) monkfish fillets, cubed
5$\frac{1}{2}$oz (150g) salmon steaks or fillets, cubed
5$\frac{1}{2}$oz (150g) tuna steaks, cubed
grated zest and juice of 1 lime
2 garlic cloves, finely chopped
handful of fresh cilantro leaves, finely chopped
2in (5cm) piece of fresh ginger, finely chopped
splash of olive oil
sea salt and freshly ground black pepper

METHOD

1 If using wooden or bamboo skewers, soak in cold water for at least 30 minutes first. Put all the ingredients in a large bowl, and season with salt and pepper. Using your hands, carefully combine everything until well mixed. Keep in the refrigerator until needed.

2 Heat a cast-iron ridged grill pan until hot. Thread the fish cubes onto the skewers, alternating the 3 types of fish. Grill over high heat for about 3 minutes on each side, turning only once during cooking. Serve hot.

FREEZING INSTRUCTIONS Freeze the kebabs uncooked, but only if the fish has not been frozen before. Prepare the recipe as in Step 1 and then thread the fish onto skewers. Freeze in a sealable freezerproof container or freezer bags for up to 1 month. To serve, defrost overnight in the refrigerator, then cook on a hot cast-iron ridged grill pan for about 3 minutes on each side.

GOOD WITH Fresh green salad.

serves 4

prep 15 mins
• cook 6 mins

healthy option

soak the
skewers in cold
water for
at least 30 mins

cast-iron ridged
grill pan
• wooden
skewers

Pan-fried lamb with green chiles

This is an especially good dish to reheat and eat—its flavors will only improve if it is prepared in advance.

INGREDIENTS

1 tbsp olive oil
1 onion, finely chopped
1 bay leaf
pinch of cumin seeds
pinch of sea salt
2 garlic cloves, finely chopped
1 fresh jalapeño chile pepper, seeded and finely chopped
2lb (900g) lean lamb, cut into bite-sized pieces
1 tbsp all-purpose flour
$2\frac{1}{4}$ cups (560ml) hot vegetable or chicken stock
3–4 green bird's-eye (Thai) chiles, left whole
juice of $\frac{1}{2}$ lemon

METHOD

1 Heat the oil in a large, deep frying pan. Add the onion, bay leaf, cumin seeds, and a pinch of salt, and sauté gently until soft. Stir in the garlic and chopped chile, and cook for a few seconds more.

2 Now add the lamb, and cook until nicely browned on the outside, then stir in the flour. Pour in a little of the stock, and increase the heat.

3 Bring to a boil. Add the remaining stock and the whole chiles. Simmer for 20 minutes, or until the lamb is cooked and the sauce has thickened. Stir in the lemon juice, and serve.

FREEZING INSTRUCTIONS Let stand to cool completely, then transfer to a sealable freezerproof container, making sure the meat is completely covered by the sauce. Freeze for up to 3 months. To serve, defrost in the refrigerator overnight, then reheat in a microwave on high for 2–3 minutes, stir, and heat for 2–3 minutes more. Let stand for 5 minutes before serving.

serves 4

prep 5 mins
• cook 30 mins

Chicken and chile burgers

These zingy burgers are perfect for anyone who likes their chicken with a bit of spice.

INGREDIENTS

1 onion, peeled and quartered
4 skinless, boneless chicken breasts
2 garlic cloves, peeled and halved
2 fresh hot red chiles, seeded
handful of fresh cilantro, chopped
sea salt and freshly ground black pepper
1 tbsp all-purpose flour
1 egg

METHOD

1 Put the onion, chicken, garlic, chiles, and cilantro into a food processor. Season with salt and pepper, and pulse until combined—be careful not to turn it into a paste. Pour the mixture out into a bowl, and mix in the flour and egg.

2 Using your hands, roll $1/4$ of the mixture into a ball, then flatten into a burger. Repeat until all the mixture has been used. Chill for 30 minutes, or until firm.

3 Heat the grill until hot. Grill the burgers over medium heat for 8–10 minutes on each side, until golden and cooked through.

FREEZING INSTRUCTIONS Freeze the burgers either uncooked or cooked and cooled. Layer them between sheets of wax paper, then wrap in a plastic freezer bag and freeze for up to 3 months. To serve, remove from the freezer bag and defrost overnight in the refrigerator. If uncooked, grill as per Step 3. If cooked, reheat in a microwave on high for 2–3 minutes, turn, and heat for 2–3 minutes more, or until piping hot. Let stand for 5 minutes before serving.

GOOD WITH Lemon mayonnaise and fresh tomato slices.

serves 4

prep 10 mins,
plus chilling
• cook 20 mins

healthy option

food processor

Fish sticks with chunky tartar sauce

This is a simple but delicious way to enjoy fresh fish and is guaranteed to be loved by old and young alike.

INGREDIENTS
1½lb (675g) thick-cut, skinless white fish fillets, such as
   haddock, sustainable cod, or pollack
1–2 tbsp all-purpose flour
1 large egg, lightly beaten
1 cup toasted homemade bread crumbs
½ cup freshly grated fresh Parmesan cheese
sea salt and freshly ground black pepper
about 3 tbsp prepared tartar sauce
1 tsp capers, rinsed, drained, and chopped
3 gherkins, drained and finely chopped

METHOD
1 Preheat the oven to 400°F (200°C). Cut the fish fillets into thick, even strips about 1in (2.5cm) wide—you should end up with about 20 "sticks."

2 Put the flour and egg onto separate plates. Mix the bread crumbs with the Parmesan cheese, and season with salt and pepper. Dredge the fish in the flour, then dip in the egg to coat. Use the bread crumb mixture to coat each of the fish sticks. Coat them well, because this protects the fish while it's cooking.

3 Place the fish sticks on a lightly oiled baking sheet without crowding, and bake for 10–15 minutes, turning once, until golden on the outside and opaque throughout. (Alternatively, fry the fish sticks, a few at a time, in a little peanut oil.)

4 Spoon the tartar sauce into a bowl, and stir in the capers and gherkins. Serve with the hot fish sticks.

FREEZING INSTRUCTIONS Let stand to cool completely, then layer between sheets of wax paper, seal in a plastic freezer bag, and freeze for up to 3 months. To serve, remove from the freezer bag, defrost in the refrigerator overnight, then fry for a couple of minutes on each side until warmed through. Alternatively, reheat in a microwave on medium for 1–2 minutes, turn, and heat for 1–2 minutes more. Let stand for 5 minutes before serving with the tartar sauce. Rather than freezing the tartar sauce, prepare it on the day you wish to serve the recipe.

GOOD WITH French fries or on a roll.

serves 4

prep 15 mins
• cook 10 mins

food processor

Seared herbed chicken with green herb sauce

The crumb crust seals in the juices, keeping the chicken succulent.

INGREDIENTS

4 skinless, boneless chicken breasts
salt and freshly ground black pepper
$1/2$ cup all-purpose flour
$2^1/2$ cups fresh bread crumbs
1 cup freshly grated Parmesan cheese
2 tbsp chopped thyme
2 tbsp chopped parsley
2 large eggs, lightly beaten
$1/4$ cup olive oil
$1/4$ cup vegetable oil

For the green herb sauce

1 large egg, plus 2 egg yolks
2 tbsp white wine vinegar
1 tbsp Dijon mustard
$1^1/4$ cups vegetable oil
sea salt and freshly ground black pepper
2 tbsp chopped basil, dill, parsley, or chives

METHOD

1 For the sauce, combine the egg, yolks, vinegar, and mustard in a blender. With the machine running, gradually add the oil to make a thick and creamy mayonnaise. Season with salt and pepper. Transfer to a bowl and stir in the herbs.

2 Lightly pound the chicken breasts to an even thickness and season with salt and pepper. Spread the flour in a shallow dish. Mix the bread crumbs, Parmesan cheese, thyme, and parsley in a shallow bowl. Beat the eggs in another bowl. Coat the chicken in the flour, shaking off the excess. Dip in the eggs, then coat with the breadcrumb mixture.

3 Heat the olive and vegetable oils in a large frying pan over medium-high heat until simmering. Add the chicken and cook, turning once, until golden brown, about 10 minutes. Transfer to paper towels to drain briefly. Serve hot with the sauce on the side.

FREEZING INSTRUCTIONS Let stand to cool completely, then wrap in wax paper and a double wrapping of plastic wrap, and freeze for up to 2 months. To serve, remove from the wrap and defrost in the refrigerator overnight. Reheat on an oiled baking tray in an oven preheated to 350°F (180°C) for 40 minutes, or until piping hot. Alternatively, reheat in a microwave on high for 3–4 minutes, turn, and heat for 3–4 minutes more. Let stand for 5 minutes before serving. Prepare the sauce fresh on the day you wish to serve the chicken.

serves 6

prep 20 mins
• cook 20–30 mins

food processor
or blender

Thai crab cakes

Served with a salad, these make a delicious lunch or light dinner.

INGREDIENTS
1lb (450g) white crabmeat
$^1/_2$ cup finely chopped green beans
1 fresh hot green or red chile, seeded and minced
1 tbsp Thai fish sauce
1 tbsp finely chopped Chinese or garlic chives
2 Kaffir lime leaves, cut into wafer-
    thin slices, or grated zest of 1 lime
1 large egg white, lightly beaten
all-purpose flour, for coating, plus more for the baking sheet
vegetable oil, for deep-frying

METHOD
1 Flake the crabmeat into a bowl, picking it over carefully to remove any small, sharp pieces of shell. Add the green beans, chile, fish sauce, chives, and lime leaves, and mix together.

2 Add the egg white, stirring to bind the mixture. Dust your hands with flour and shape the mixture into 18 small balls. Flatten them slightly into cakes. Place on a floured baking sheet, spaced slightly apart so they don't stick together, and refrigerate for 1 hour or until firm.

3 Preheat the oven to 200°F (95°C). Pour enough oil into a large, deep frying pan to come about 1in (2.5cm) up the sides, and heat to 325°F (160°C). In batches, dredge the crab cakes in flour, shaking off the excess. Fry for about 3 minutes, until golden. Transfer to a baking sheet lined with paper towels, and keep warm in the oven.

FREEZING INSTRUCTIONS Let stand to cool completely, then layer between sheets of wax paper, seal in a plastic freezer bag, and freeze for up to 1 month. To serve, remove from the freezer bag and defrost in the refrigerator overnight. Reheat in a microwave on medium for 1–2 minutes, turn, and heat for 1–2 minutes more, or until piping hot. Let stand for 5 minutes before serving.

GOOD WITH Spicy dipping sauce and a Thai noodle salad or broken over a leafy green salad.

makes 20

prep 30 mins,
plus chilling
• cook 20 mins

Stuffed eggplants

Turkish legend says these eggplants once made a holy man faint, so they are called *Imam Bayildi* ("the holy man swooned").

INGREDIENTS
4 small eggplants
6 tbsp olive oil
2 large onions, finely sliced
3 garlic cloves, minced
1 tbsp ground coriander
1 tbsp ground cumin
1 tsp ground turmeric
$^1/_2$ tsp ground cardamom
2 x 14.5oz (411g) cans chopped tomatoes
$^1/_2$ cup golden raisins
2 tbsp chopped cilantro
1 tbsp chopped mint
1 tbsp chopped parsley

METHOD
1 Preheat the oven to 350°F (180°C). Cut the eggplants in half lengthwise and score the flesh of each in a crosshatch pattern with a sharp knife.

2 Brush the flesh with 4 tablespoons of the oil. Place, cut sides up, in a roasting pan. Bake in the oven for 30–35 minutes, or until tender.

3 Let the eggplants cool. Scoop out and reserve the flesh, leaving a $^1/_4$in (6mm) shell, being careful not to split the skins. Place on a serving platter.

4 Heat the remaining 2 tablespoons of the oil in a large, heavy-bottomed saucepan over medium heat. Add the onion and garlic and cook, stirring occasionally, about 5 minutes until softened. Add the coriander, cumin, turmeric, and cardamom and stir about 1 minute, until fragrant.

5 Stir in the tomatoes and their juices and bring to a boil. Reduce the heat and simmer for about 30 minutes, stirring occasionally, until reduced and thickened. Stir in the reserved eggplant flesh and raisins and cook for 10 minutes more. Let cool, then stir in the cilantro, mint, and parsley.

6 Spoon the mixture into the eggplant shells, and refrigerate for at least 1 day before serving.

FREEZING INSTRUCTIONS Once filled, let stand to cool completely and transfer to a sealable freezerproof container. Freeze for up to 1 month. To serve, defrost in the refrigerator overnight, then bring to room temperature before serving.

GOOD WITH Herb salad and Greek yogurt.

serves 4

prep 20 mins,
plus cooling
and chilling
• cook 1 hr
10 mins

healthy option

chill for at
least 3 hrs, or
overnight

Lamb and mint burgers

Fresh ginger and garlic add a twist to this classic flavor combination.

INGREDIENTS

1 tbsp olive oil
1 tbsp butter
1 onion, finely chopped
2 garlic cloves, finely chopped
1in (2.5cm) piece of fresh ginger, finely grated
sea salt and freshly ground black pepper
1½lb (675g) ground lamb
handful of fresh mint leaves, finely chopped
vegetable oil, for frying

METHOD

1 In a large frying pan, heat the oil and butter over low heat. Add the onion and cook for 5 minutes, or until soft. Add the garlic, ginger, a pinch of salt, and pepper to taste. Remove from the heat and let cool.

2 Put the lamb in a large bowl and add the cooled onion mixture and the mint. Season with salt and pepper, then mix together until well combined—this is best done using your hands. Form large balls with the mixture, and flatten to make burgers. Place the burgers on a plate, and refrigerate until firm, if time permits.

3 Heat 1½ tablespoons of vegetable oil in a large frying pan. Cook the burgers for 5–6 minutes on each side until cooked through and no longer pink. Alternatively, grill on a hot griddle, cast-iron ridged grill pan, or barbecue grill. Serve hot.

FREEZING INSTRUCTIONS Freeze the burgers either uncooked or cooked and cooled. Layer them between sheets of wax paper, then seal in a plastic freezer bag and freeze for up to 3 months. To serve, remove from the freezer bag and defrost overnight in the refrigerator. If uncooked, cook as per Step 3. If cooked, reheat in a microwave on high for 2–3 minutes, turn, and heat for 2–3 minutes more, or until piping hot. Let stand for 5 minutes before serving.

GOOD WITH Roasted butternut squash and arugula.

serves 4

prep 10 mins,
plus chilling
• cook 20 mins

Eggplant parmigiana

This is one of Italy's most popular dishes and a great choice for vegetarians.

INGREDIENTS

$1/2$ cup all-purpose flour
2 large eggs
salt and freshly ground black pepper
2 large eggplants, cut lengthwise into $1/2$in slices
$1/4$ cup olive oil, plus more as needed
2 cups tomato sauce
10oz (300g) mozzarella, drained and sliced
$1/2$ cup grated Parmesan cheese
$1/3$ cup chopped basil

METHOD

1 Preheat the oven to 325°F (160°C). Spread the flour on a plate. Beat the eggs in a shallow bowl and season with salt and pepper. One at a time, dredge each eggplant slice in the flour, shaking off the excess, then dip it in the eggs and let the excess drip back into the bowl. Repeat with the remaining slices.

2 Heat the oil in a large skillet over a medium heat. Working in batches, if necessary, fry the eggplant slices for about 5 minutes on each side, or until golden. Drain well on paper towels.

3 Layer the tomato sauce, eggplant slices, mozzarella, Parmesan cheese, and basil in a shallow casserole dish, seasoning each layer with salt and pepper, and finishing with a layer of tomato sauce and the cheeses.

4 Place the dish on a baking sheet. Bake for 30 minutes, or until the sauce is bubbling and the cheese has melted. Serve hot.

FREEZING INSTRUCTIONS Assemble in a freezerproof baking dish. Let stand to cool completely, then double wrap in plastic wrap and freeze for up to 3 months. To serve, defrost in its container in the refrigerator overnight, remove the plastic wrap and reheat in an oven preheated to 350°F (180°C) for 30–40 minutes, or until piping hot. Alternatively, reheat portions in a microwave on medium for 2–3 minutes, agitate, and heat for 2–3 minutes more, or until piping hot. Let stand for 5 minutes before serving.

GOOD WITH A simple salad.

serves 4

prep 40 mins
• cook 30 mins

Moussaka

This recipe makes individual servings, which are easier to freeze.

INGREDIENTS

2 large eggplants, cut into $^1/_4$in (5mm) rounds
salt and freshly ground black pepper
8 tbsp olive oil
1 large onion, chopped
1lb (450g) ground lamb
$^1/_2$ cup hearty red wine
2 cups canned crushed tomatoes
$^1/_2$ cup lamb or beef stock
2 tsp dried oregano
1 tsp sugar

1lb (450g) baking potatoes, such as Russet
    Burbank, cut into $^1/_4$in (5mm) slices
$^1/_4$ cup freshly grated Parmesan cheese
$^1/_4$ cup plain dried bread crumbs

For the topping
1 cup plain Greek-style yogurt
3 large eggs
1 tbsp cornstarch
$^1/_2$ cup cottage cheese
$^1/_2$ cup crumbled feta cheese

METHOD

1 Toss the eggplant with 2 tablespoons of salt in a colander. Let stand in the sink to drain for 30 minutes. Rinse well under cold running water. Drain and pat dry.

2 Meanwhile, heat 2 tablespoons of the oil in a large saucepan over medium heat. Add the onion and cook, stirring occasionally, until softened, about 5 minutes. Add the lamb and increase the heat. Cook, breaking up the meat with a spoon, about 5 minutes, until it loses its raw look. Pour off excess fat.

3 Add the wine and boil for 2 minutes. Stir in the tomatoes, stock, 1 teaspoon of the oregano, and sugar. Season with salt and pepper. Simmer, uncovered, over medium heat, stirring occasionally, for 30 minutes, or until the meat sauce is quite thick.

4 Preheat the broiler. Brush the eggplant on both sides with the remaining 6 tablespoons of oil. In batches, broil the eggplant, turning once, about 5 minutes, until golden brown on both sides. Boil the potato slices in a large saucepan of lightly salted water for about 8 minutes, until just tender. Drain.

5 To make the topping, whisk the yogurt, eggs, and cornstarch together until smooth, then whisk in the cottage cheese and feta cheese.

6 Preheat the oven to 350°F (180°C). Lightly oil 6 individual freezer-to-oven casseroles. In each casserole, starting with the eggplant, alternate 2 layers each of eggplant and meat sauce. Top with the potato slices, then the yogurt sauce. Mix the Parmesan cheese, bread crumbs, and the remaining 1 teaspoon of oregano and sprinkle over the potatoes.

7 Bake for 45 minutes, or until golden brown and bubbling. Serve while the moussaka is hot.

FREEZING INSTRUCTIONS Let stand to cool completely in their dishes, then double wrap in plastic wrap and freeze for up to 3 months. To serve, defrost in the containers in the refrigerator overnight, remove the plastic wrap, cover with foil, and reheat in an oven preheated to 350°F (180°C) for 30–40 minutes, or until piping hot.

serves 4

prep 30 mins,
plus standing
• cook 1 hr
30 mins

6 x 3½–4in
(8–10cm)
ovenproof
casserole dishes

Coquilles St. Jacques

This scallop dish is impressive for entertaining.

INGREDIENTS

8 large sea scallops
$^1/_4$ cup dry white wine
1 x 3in (7.5cm) piece of celery
small sprig of thyme
4 whole black peppercorns
1 bay leaf
8oz (225g) white mushrooms
juice of $^1/_2$ lemon
3 tbsp butter
1 tbsp all-purpose flour

$^1/_4$ cup heavy cream or crème fraîche
$^1/_2$ cup shredded Gruyère cheese

For the piped potatoes
1lb (450g) baking potatoes, peeled and
   cut into chunks
2 tbsp butter
large pinch of freshly grated nutmeg
salt and freshly ground black pepper
3 large egg yolks

METHOD

1 Boil the potatoes in lightly salted water about 20 minutes, until tender. Drain and mash with the butter and nutmeg, and season with salt and pepper. Stir over low heat about 2 minutes. Remove from the heat and cool slightly. Beat in the egg yolks. Transfer to a pastry bag fitted with a $^1/_2$in (1cm) plain tip.

2 Preheat the oven to 425°F (220°C). Bring the scallops, $^2/_3$ cup water, wine, celery, thyme, peppercorns, bay leaf, and a large pinch of salt to a boil over low heat. Cover and simmer for 1–2 minutes, just until the scallops look opaque on the outside. Strain over a bowl and reserve the cooking liquid.

3 Simmer the mushrooms and lemon juice in a small covered saucepan over medium-low heat about 5 minutes, or until tender. Season with salt and pepper. Uncover and boil over high heat until the liquid is evaporated. Add to the scallops.

4 To make the sauce, melt 1 tablespoon of the butter in a saucepan over low heat. Whisk in the flour and cook for 1 minute, whisking constantly. Whisk in the reserved liquid and whisk until simmering and thickened. Simmer, whisking often, until slightly reduced. Remove from the heat and stir in the cream and $^1/_4$ cup of the Gruyère cheese. Cut each scallop into 2 or 3 pieces and stir into the sauce with the mushrooms. Season with salt and pepper.

5 Spoon the mixture into each shell or ramekin and sprinkle the remaining Gruyère cheese on top. Pipe a generous border of potato around the edge of each shell. Dot with the remaining butter. Bake for about 15 minutes, or until golden. Serve hot.

FREEZING INSTRUCTIONS Assemble in freezerproof dishes. Let stand to cool, then double wrap in plastic wrap and freeze for up to 3 months. To serve, defrost in the container in the refrigerator overnight, remove the plastic wrap, and reheat in a microwave on medium for 2–3 minutes, agitate, and heat for 2–3 minutes more, or until piping hot.

serves 4

prep 20 mins
• cook 50 mins

4 scallop shells
or ramekins
• piping bag

Shepherd's Pie

Traditionally, this pie was used for leftover roast meat and potatoes, but is now more commonly made with ground lamb.

INGREDIENTS

2½lb (1.1kg) potatoes
2 tbsp butter
sea salt and freshly ground
   black pepper
6 tbsp olive oil
3 large onions, diced
4 large carrots, diced
2½lb (1.1kg) ground lamb
6 garlic cloves, chopped
2 tsp dried oregano
3 x 14oz (400g) cans diced tomatoes
9oz (250g) frozen peas

METHOD

1 Put the potatoes in a pot of boiling water and cook for 15 minutes, until soft. Drain, then mash well. Add the butter and mash again until creamy. Season with salt and pepper, then set aside.

2 Meanwhile, heat the oil in a large heavy-based saucepan over medium heat, add the onions and carrots, and cook for 5 minutes or until the onions are starting to soften. Add the lamb and cook, stirring constantly, for 10 minutes or until no longer pink. Add the garlic and oregano, cook for 1 minute, then stir in the tomatoes and bring to a boil.

3 Add the peas, season with salt and pepper, then return to a boil and lower the heat. Simmer for 20 minutes, stirring occasionally.

4 Preheat the oven to 350°F (180°C). Pour a 1½in (3.5cm) layer of lamb sauce into 2 large baking dishes (4 portions per dish) and top with the mashed potatoes. Bake for 25 minutes or until brown on top and piping hot inside.

FREEZING INSTRUCTIONS Assemble in freezerproof baking dishes. Let stand to cool completely, then double wrap in plastic wrap and freeze for up to 3 months. To serve, defrost in the containers in the refrigerator overnight, and reheat in a microwave on high for 3–4 minutes, agitate, and heat for 3–4 minutes more, or until piping hot. Let stand for 5 minutes before serving.

GOOD WITH A green salad or minted peas.

serves 8

prep 30 mins
• cook 20 mins

Vegetarian leek and mushroom lasagna

Mushrooms and chiles add a meaty texture and a pleasant heat to this dish.

INGREDIENTS

$^1/_2$ cup olive oil
4 leeks, cut into $^1/_4$in (5mm) slices
1$^1/_4$lb (550g) cremini mushrooms, sliced and
  9oz (250g) cremini mushrooms, grated
2–3 red chiles, seeded and finely chopped
6 garlic cloves, chopped
$^2/_3$ cup dry white wine
small handful of fresh thyme leaves
2 tbsp all-purpose flour

3 cups milk
12oz (350g) medium-sharp Cheddar
  cheese, grated
6 tomatoes, coarsely chopped
sea salt and freshly ground
  black pepper
1lb (450g) oven-ready lasagna noodles
2 tomatoes, sliced

METHOD

1 Heat the oil in a large heavy-based saucepan, add the leeks, and sauté over low heat, for 5 minutes or until starting to soften. Stir in the mushrooms and cook, stirring frequently, for 5 minutes or until they release their juices. Add the chiles and garlic and cook for 1 minute. Pour in the wine, raise the heat, and allow to bubble for 3 minutes while the alcohol evaporates.

2 Stir in the thyme, then add the flour and mix well. Add a little of the milk, mix well, then add the rest of the milk and cook for 5 minutes, stirring frequently. Add almost all the cheese (reserve some for the topping), remove from heat, and combine well. Add the coarsely chopped tomatoes and season with salt and pepper.

3 Preheat the oven to 350°F (180°C). Put a $^1/_2$in (1cm) layer of the mixture in the bottom of a large freezerproof baking pan, then cover evenly with 1 layer of the lasagna noodles. Pour in another layer of sauce and cover with lasagna noodles. Repeat the process until all the sauce is used up—you need to finish with a layer of sauce. Top with the remaining cheese and the sliced tomatoes. Bake for 30–40 minutes or until browned on top and piping hot inside.

FREEZING INSTRUCTIONS Assemble in a freezerproof baking dish. Let stand to cool completely, then double wrap in plastic wrap and freeze for up to 3 months. To serve, defrost in its container in the refrigerator overnight, remove the plastic wrap, cover with foil, and reheat in an oven preheated to 350°F (180°C) for 30–40 minutes, or until piping hot. Alternatively, reheat portions in a microwave on medium for 2–3 minutes, agitate, and heat for 2–3 minutes more, or until piping hot. Let stand for 5 minutes before serving.

serves 8

prep 25 mins
• cook 20 mins

Spinach and mushroom crêpes

Savory crêpes are great for lunch, dinner, or brunch.

INGREDIENTS

1¼ cups whole milk
scant 1 cup all-purpose flour
1 large egg plus 1 large egg yolk
1 tbsp light olive oil or melted butter, plus
   extra for frying
pinch of salt

For the filling
2 tbsp butter
7oz (200g) mushrooms, chopped

1 x 10oz (280g) box frozen chopped
   spinach
1¾ cups Béchamel sauce, thawed
pinch of grated nutmeg
salt and freshly ground black pepper
¾ cup shredded sharp
   Cheddar cheese
½ tsp dry mustard
2 ripe tomatoes, sliced
3 tbsp grated Parmesan cheese

METHOD

1 To make the crêpes, process all of the ingredients in a blender until smooth. Let the mixture stand for 30 minutes.

2 Lightly grease the frying pan with melted butter. Add about 3 tablespoons of the batter to the pan, and tilt and swirl the pan so the batter covers the bottom. Cook until the underside is golden brown. Turn the crêpe and cook until the other side is golden. Transfer to a plate. Repeat with the remaining batter, buttering the pan as needed. You should have 12 crêpes. Separate the crêpes with pieces of wax paper.

3 To make the filling, melt the butter in a frying pan over medium heat. Add the mushrooms and cook 6 minutes. Transfer to a bowl. Add the spinach and ¼ cup of the Béchamel sauce. Season with nutmeg, salt, and pepper.

4 Preheat the oven to 375°F (190°C). Divide the filling among the crêpes. Roll them up and place in a shallow buttered baking dish. Stir the Cheddar cheese and mustard into the remaining sauce and season with salt and pepper. Spread over the crêpes. Arrange the tomato on top and sprinkle with the Parmesan cheese. Bake for 30 minutes, or until bubbling and browned.

FREEZING INSTRUCTIONS Freeze this dish uncooked. Assemble in a freezerproof baking dish, double wrap in plastic wrap, and freeze for up to 3 months. To serve, defrost overnight in the refrigerator, remove the plastic wrap, cover with foil, and reheat in an oven preheated to 350°F (180°C) for 30–40 minutes, or until piping hot.

serves 4

prep 30 mins
• cook 1 hr
10 mins

6–8in (15–20cm)
heavy
frying pan

Cheesy potato and mushroom gratin

Vegetarians (and everyone else!) will love this hearty, comforting bake.

INGREDIENTS

1 tbsp butter
4^1/$_2$oz (125g) mushrooms, sliced
2 garlic cloves, finely chopped
a few sprigs of fresh thyme,
    leaves picked
2lb (900g) all-purpose waxy potatoes,
    peeled and thinly sliced
1 cup Gruyère cheese, shredded
sea salt and freshly ground
    black pepper

METHOD

1 Preheat the oven to 400°F (200°C). Heat the butter in a frying pan, then add the mushrooms and cook for a few minutes until soft. Add the garlic and thyme, and cook for 1 minute longer.

2 Arrange a layer of potatoes in the bottom of a baking dish, then top with some of the cheese and mushrooms. Season each layer with a pinch of salt and pepper as you go. Continue layering until you have used all of the ingredients, finishing with potatoes, and a sprinkling of cheese on top.

3 Bake in the oven for 25 minutes, or until golden on top and bubbly-hot.

FREEZING INSTRUCTIONS Assemble in a freezerproof baking dish. Let stand to cool completely, then double wrap in plastic wrap and freeze for up to 3 months. To serve, defrost in its container in the refrigerator overnight, remove the plastic wrap, and reheat in a microwave on medium for 3–4 minutes, agitate, and heat for 3–4 minutes more, or until piping hot. Let stand for 5 minutes before serving.

GOOD WITH A crisp green salad.

serves 4

prep 10 mins
• cook 30 mins

Vegetarian moussaka

A healthy and delicious take on this famous Greek dish.

INGREDIENTS

1 tbsp olive oil
1 onion, finely chopped
sea salt and freshly ground
    black pepper
1 tsp dried mint leaves
3 tsp dried oregano
1 x 15oz (425g) can aduki beans, drained and rinsed
1 x 28oz (800g) can ground tomatoes or tomato purée
$^3/_4$ cup pine nuts
freshly ground black pepper
9oz (250g) Greek-style plain yogurt
1 large egg

METHOD

1 Preheat the oven to 400°F (200°C). Heat the oil in a saucepan over low heat. Add the onion and a pinch of sea salt, and cook gently for about 5 minutes, or until soft. Stir in the mint and 1 teaspoon of the dried oregano.

2 Add the beans, tomatoes, and pine nuts, and bring to a boil. Reduce the heat to low, and simmer gently for 15–20 minutes until thickened. Season well with salt and pepper.

3 Spoon the bean mixture into a baking dish. Mix together the yogurt, egg, and the remaining 2 teaspoons of oregano. Spoon evenly over the top of the bean mixture. Bake for 15–20 minutes until the top is golden, puffed, and set. Serve hot.

FREEZING INSTRUCTIONS Assemble in a freezerproof baking dish. Let stand to cool completely, then double wrap in plastic wrap and freeze for up to 3 months. To serve, defrost in its container in the refrigerator overnight, remove the plastic wrap, cover with foil, and reheat in an oven preheated to 350°F (180°C) for 30–50 minutes, or until piping hot.

GOOD WITH A crisp green salad.

serves 4

prep 15 mins
• cook 30 mins

healthy option

Shepherdless pie

Aduki beans make a satisfying vegetarian version of this potato-topped pie.

INGREDIENTS

1½lb (675g) Russet Burbank potatoes,
   peeled and quartered
1 tbsp butter, plus extra for dotting on top
1 tbsp olive oil
1 onion, finely chopped
1 bay leaf
sea salt and freshly ground
   black pepper
3 celery stalks, finely chopped

3 carrots, finely chopped
7oz (200g) mushrooms, coarsely chopped
handful of fresh thyme sprigs, leaves picked
   (reserve some for garnish)
splash of soy sauce
1 x 15oz (425g) can aduki beans, drained
   and rinsed
⅔ cup hot vegetable stock

METHOD

1 Preheat the oven to 400°F (200°C). To make the topping, boil the potatoes in a saucepan of salted water for 15–20 minutes, or until soft. Drain the potatoes, then mash. Add the butter, and mash again. Set aside and keep warm.

2 Meanwhile, heat the oil in a large frying pan over low heat. Add the onion, bay leaf, and a pinch of salt, and cook for 5 minutes until the onion is soft. Add the celery and carrots and cook for another 5 minutes.

3 Pulse the mushrooms several times in a food processor—you want them finely chopped, but not mushy. Add these to the pan along with the thyme and soy sauce, and cook for 5–10 minutes, until the mushrooms begin to release their juices. Add the aduki beans, and season well with salt and pepper. Pour in the stock, bring to a boil, reduce the heat slightly, and simmer for 5 minutes.

4 Scrape into a baking dish and top with the reserved mashed potatoes. Dot with butter, and bake until the topping is crisp and golden. Serve hot.

FREEZING INSTRUCTIONS Assemble in a freezerproof baking dish. Let stand to cool completely, then double wrap in plastic wrap and freeze for up to 3 months. To serve, defrost in its container in the refrigerator overnight, and reheat in a microwave on medium for 3–4 minutes, agitate, and heat for 3–4 minutes more, or until piping hot. Let stand for 5 minutes before serving.

serves 4

**prep 15 mins
• cook 30 mins**

healthy option

food processor

Haddock with cheese sauce

With a layer of freshly-cooked spinach under the poached haddock, this dish is a colorful one-pot meal.

INGREDIENTS
1¹/₂lb (675g) skinless haddock or cod fillet, cut into 4 serving pieces
1¹/₄ cups whole milk
²/₃ cup bottled clam juice
9oz (250g) fresh spinach, well washed, stemmed, and chopped
salt and freshly ground black pepper
pinch of grated nutmeg
2 tbsp butter, plus more for the dish
2 tbsp all-purpose flour
1 cup shredded Cheddar cheese
1 cup fresh whole wheat bread crumbs
¹/₂ cup freshly grated Parmesan cheese
2 tbsp chopped parsley

METHOD
1 Bring the haddock, milk, and clam juice to a boil in a frying pan over medium heat. Reduce the heat to low, cover, and simmer for 6–8 minutes, or until the fish is opaque.

2 Meanwhile, put the spinach in a medium saucepan. Cover and cook over medium-low heat for 3 minutes, or until wilted. Season with salt, pepper, and the nutmeg. Spread the spinach in a buttered shallow ovenproof dish. Arrange the fish over the spinach, leaving the cooking liquid in the pan. Cover with aluminum foil to keep the fish warm.

3 Melt the butter over low heat. Whisk in the flour and let bubble for 1 minute without browning. Whisk in the poaching liquid and bring to a boil over medium heat, whisking often. Stir in the Cheddar cheese until melted, then season with salt and pepper. Pour the sauce over the fish and spinach. Mix the bread crumbs, Parmesan cheese, and parsley together and sprinkle over the sauce.

4 Position a broiler rack about 6in (15cm) from the heat and preheat the broiler. Broil about 2 minutes, or until the topping is golden brown. Serve immediately.

FREEZING INSTRUCTIONS Assemble in a freezerproof baking dish. Let stand to cool completely, then double wrap in plastic wrap and freeze for up to 3 months. To serve, defrost in its container in the refrigerator overnight, and reheat in a microwave on medium for 3–4 minutes, agitate, and heat for 3–4 minutes more, or until piping hot. Let stand for 5 minutes before serving.

serves 4

prep 25 mins
• cook 25 mins

Make basic pizza dough

A quick dough mixture using dried yeast—the quantities given here make 4 thin-crust Italian-style pizzas.

1 Sift 1lb 2oz (500g) of all-purpose flour into a bowl, add a pinch of salt, and a package of dried yeast. Slowly add 12fl oz (360ml) warm water and mix until it comes together. Add 2fl oz (60ml) of olive oil, and continue to mix until it forms a soft dough.

2 Place the dough on a floured surface, and knead firmly, using the heel of your hand, folding the dough over as you go. Do this for about 10 minutes, until it becomes soft and spongy.

3 Put the dough in a bowl, cover with plastic wrap or a dish towel, and leave in a warm place (try leaving the bowl on the stove above a preheated oven) for 30–40 minutes, or until it has doubled in size.

4 Roll the dough out onto a floured surface and knead with your knuckles to knock out the air. Divide the dough into quarters and roll each piece thinly to about 10in (25cm) in diameter.

Make shortcrust pastry

Baked shortcrust pastry has a crisp and firm, but light, texture. This is the one to start with for anyone new to pastry-making.

1 Sift 6oz (175g) all-purpose flour and a pinch of salt into a large bowl. Add 3oz (85g) chilled, cubed butter or margarine. Lightly stir the butter to coat it in the flour.

2 Quickly and lightly rub the butter or margarine into the flour with your fingertips until the mixture resembles coarse bread crumbs. Try to incorporate all the flour.

3 Sprinkle in 2 tbsp of iced water and stir with a wooden spoon or use your hands to gently mix until the dough comes together (the less you handle the dough, the lighter the pastry will be).

4 Shape the dough into a ball (or balls), wrap it in plastic wrap, and chill for at least 2 hours. Allowing the gluten and flour to relax during chilling will prevent the dough from shrinking in the hot oven.

Line a tart pan

Once your pastry dough is made, and has been chilled for the gluten to relax, follow these simple steps to line a pan of any size or shape.

1 Roll out the pastry (see previous page for quantities and method) on a lightly floured surface, to a circle about 2in (5cm) wider than the tart pan. The pastry should be fairly thin.

2 Carefully drape the pastry over a rolling pin and gently lay it over the tart pan, so the pastry hangs over the edge.

3 Gently ease the pastry into the sides of the pan using your fingertips or knuckles, being careful not to tear it.

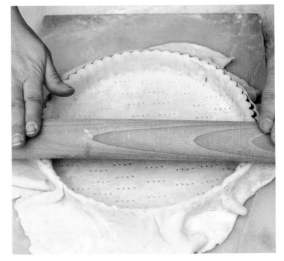

4 Once in place, prick the base all over with a fork, then roll a rolling pin over the top of the pan to remove the pastry that hangs over the edge. Put in the refrigerator to chill for 30 minutes.

Blind bake a tart shell

Tart shells should be prebaked unfilled if they will contain moist fillings, such as egg or cream, to prevent them from becoming soggy.

1 Fit the pastry in the pan (see opposite) and ensure that you prick the bottom with a fork. This will allow trapped air to escape during baking, helping to prevent a soggy base.

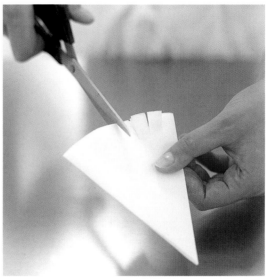

2 Cut out a circle of parchment paper slightly larger than the pan. Fold the parchment in half 3 times to make a triangular shape, and clip the edges at regular intervals with scissors.

3 Place the parchment circle into the pan, and fill it with an even layer of dried beans or ceramic baking beans. Bake the shell in a preheated 400°F (200°C) oven for 10 minutes.

4 Remove the beans and parchment when cool enough to handle. Return the shell to the oven for another 5 minutes for partially baked, or 10–15 minutes for fully baked pastry. Cool on a wire rack.

Pizza with tomatoes, olives, and capers

Passata, or sieved tomatoes, is ideal for pizza bases, but if you cannot get any, try blending canned tomatoes instead.

INGREDIENTS
1 ball pizza dough (see page 156)
all-purpose flour, for dusting
semolina flour or cornmeal, to sprinkle
2–3 tbsp ground tomatoes or tomato purée or sauce
3 tomatoes, sliced
handful of pitted black olives
1–2 tsp capers, rinsed
freshly ground black pepper

METHOD
1 Preheat the oven to 475°F (245°C). Put a heavy baking sheet in the oven to get hot. (They both need to be really hot before cooking the pizza.)

2 Place the dough on a floured surface and use a rolling pin to roll it out as thin as you can—about 10–12in (25–30cm) in diameter. Brush the hot baking sheet with oil, sprinkle with semolina, and carefully place the dough on top.

3 Spread the ground tomatoes on to the pizza crust, using the back of a spoon to smooth it out evenly. Top with the tomato slices, then scatter with the olives and capers. Bake for 10–15 minutes or until the crust is crisp and golden. Season with pepper and serve.

FREEZING INSTRUCTIONS Let stand to cool completely, then double wrap in plastic wrap and freeze for up to 1 month. To serve, defrost overnight in the refrigerator, then slice, and reheat in a microwave on medium for 1–2 minutes, turn, and heat for 1–2 minutes more, or until piping hot. Let stand for 5 minutes before serving.

serves 4

**prep 10 mins,
plus making
the dough
• cook 15 mins**

Pissaladière

This onion-and-olive pizza is a real crowd pleaser.

INGREDIENTS

1²/₃ cups bread flour, plus more
   for kneading
1 tsp instant yeast
1 tsp brown sugar
1 tsp salt
1 tbsp olive oil

For the topping

¹/₄ cup olive oil
2lb (900g) onions, finely sliced
3 garlic cloves, sliced
1 tsp herbes de Provence
1 sprig thyme
1 bay leaf
2 x 2oz (56g) cans anchovies in oil (if using)
12 pitted Kalamata olives
salt and freshly ground black pepper

METHOD

1 To make the dough, stir the flour, yeast, brown sugar, and salt together in a bowl. Make a well in the center and add ²/₃ cup tepid water and oil. Stir to make a soft dough, adding more water if needed.

2 Knead on a floured work surface for about 8 minutes, until smooth and elastic. Shape into a ball. Place in an oiled bowl and turn to coat with oil. Cover with plastic wrap and let stand in a warm place for about 1 hour, until doubled.

3 For the topping, heat the oil in a large, heavy-bottomed casserole over low heat. Add the onions, garlic, herbs, thyme, and bay leaf. Cover and cook, stirring occasionally, adding a little water if the onions begin to stick, for about 45 minutes, until very tender. Drain in a sieve, discarding the thyme and bay leaf. Let cool.

4 Preheat the oven to 350°F (180°C). Lightly oil a 13 x 9in (33 x 23cm) nonstick jelly roll pan. Knead the dough briefly on a floured work surface. Roll into a rectangle to fit the jelly roll pan, and transfer to the pan. Prick all over with a fork.

5 Spread the onions over the dough. Drain the anchovies (if using), reserving 3 tablespoons of oil. Arrange the anchovy fillets in a crisscross pattern over the onions, and garnish with the olives. Drizzle with the reserved anchovy oil, and sprinkle with pepper.

6 Bake for about 25 minutes, until the crust is brown. Let cool slightly. Cut into serving pieces and serve warm, or cool completely.

FREEZING INSTRUCTIONS Let stand to cool in the pan, then double wrap in plastic wrap and freeze in the pan for up to 1 month. To serve, defrost in the refrigerator overnight, then reheat in a microwave on medium for 1–2 minutes, turn, and heat for 1–2 minutes more, or until piping hot. Let stand for 5 minutes before serving.

serves 4

prep 20 mins,
plus rising
• cook 1 hr
25 mins

13 x 9in
(32.5 x 23cm)
nonstick jelly
roll pan

Pizzette

Try these mini party pizzas with the toppings below, or create your own favorite combinations.

INGREDIENTS

1 ball pizza dough (see page 156)
3 tbsp pesto, homemade or store-bought
3 tbsp sun-dried tomato paste
2oz (60g) sliced salami or pepperoni, cut into strips
6 pitted Kalamata olives, halved
2oz (60g) mozzarella, cut into small slices
$1/2$ cup packed, coarsely chopped arugula leaves
2 tbsp pine nuts
extra virgin olive oil, to drizzle

METHOD

1 Preheat the oven to 425°F (220°C). Lightly oil 2 or 3 large baking sheets.

2 Knead the pizza dough on a lightly floured surface. Roll out into a thin rectangle $1/4$in (5mm) thick. Using a 3in (7.5cm) round cookie cutter, cut out 24 rounds, gathering up the dough trimmings and re-rolling as required. Transfer the rounds to the baking sheets.

3 Spread 12 rounds with the pesto and half with the sun-dried tomato paste. Top the pesto rounds with salami, olives, and mozzarella. Top the sun-dried tomato rounds with the arugula and pine nuts. Brush with olive oil, cover loosely with a clean paper towel, and let stand for 20 minutes, or until puffy.

4 Bake for 12–15 minutes, until golden brown. Serve warm.

FREEZING INSTRUCTIONS Let stand to cool completely, then double wrap in plastic wrap and freeze for up to 1 month. To serve, defrost overnight in the refrigerator, then reheat in a microwave on medium for 1–2 minutes, turn, and heat for 1–2 minutes more, or until piping hot. Let stand for 5 minutes before serving.

makes 24

prep 20 mins, plus making the dough • cook 12–15 mins

3in (7.5cm) round cookie cutter

Calzone with peppers, capers, and olives

This relative of pizza is very portable and great for lunch boxes and picnics.

INGREDIENTS
1 ball pizza dough (see page 156)
all-purpose flour, for dusting
semolina flour or cornmeal, to sprinkle
3–4 roasted red peppers from a jar, drained and chopped
handful of pitted black olives, coarsely chopped
1–2 tsp capers, rinsed
2–3 tbsp ricotta cheese or fresh mozzarella, torn into pieces
sea salt and freshly ground black pepper

METHOD
1 Preheat the oven to 475°F (245°C). Put a heavy baking sheet in the oven to get hot. (They both need to be really hot before cooking the calzone.)

2 Place the dough on a floured surface and use a rolling pin to roll it out as thin as you can—about 10–12in (25–30cm) in diameter. Brush the hot baking sheet with oil, sprinkle with semolina flour, and carefully place the dough on top.

3 Spoon the peppers, olives, capers, and ricotta cheese onto half of the dough base, leaving a ½in (1cm) border around the edge. Season well with salt and pepper. Moisten the edges of the dough with a little water, then fold in half and seal together with your fingers. Sprinkle the top with a little water, then bake for 15–20 minutes or until golden and crispy.

FREEZING INSTRUCTIONS Let stand to cool completely, then double wrap in plastic wrap and freeze for up to 1 month. To serve, defrost overnight in the refrigerator, then reheat in a microwave on medium for 1–2 minutes, turn, and heat for 1–2 minutes more, or until piping hot. Let stand for 5 minutes before serving.

makes 1

prep 15 mins, plus making the dough • cook 20 mins

Swiss chard and Gruyère cheese tart

With its subtle bitterness, Swiss chard adds character to this cheese tart.

INGREDIENTS

1 sheet prepared dough for an 8–9in (20–23cm) pie
all-purpose flour
2 large eggs, plus 1 extra yolk, lightly beaten, for egg wash
1 tbsp olive oil
1 onion, finely chopped
sea salt and freshly ground black pepper
2 garlic cloves, finely chopped
a few sprigs of fresh rosemary, leaves picked and finely chopped
1 bunch Swiss chard, about 9oz (250g), stems trimmed,
    leaves coarsely chopped
1 cup shredded Gruyère cheese
1 cup cubed or crumbled feta cheese
1 cup heavy whipping cream

METHOD

1 Preheat the oven to 400°F (200°C). Roll out the pastry on a floured work surface. Use pastry to line a tart pan with a removable bottom. Trim away the excess, line the pastry shell with parchment paper, and fill with baking beans. Bake for 15–30 minutes until the edges are golden. Remove the beans and the paper and brush the bottom of the shell with a little of the egg wash. Return to the oven for 1–2 minutes to crisp. Remove from the oven, and set aside. Reduce the oven temperature to 350°F (180°C).

2 Heat the oil in a saucepan over low heat. Add the onion and a pinch of salt, and cook gently for 5 minutes until soft. Add the garlic and rosemary, cook for a few seconds, then stir in the Swiss chard. Cook for about 5 minutes, stirring, until it wilts.

3 Spoon the onion and chard mixture into the pastry shell. Sprinkle in the Gruyère cheese, and scatter the feta cheese overtop. Season well with salt and pepper. Mix together the cream and 2 eggs until well blended, and carefully pour over the filling. Bake for 30–40 minutes until set and golden. Let stand to cool for 10 minutes before removing the sides of the pan. Serve warm or at room temperature.

FREEZING INSTRUCTIONS Let stand to cool completely, then wrap in wax paper and 2 layers of plastic wrap and freeze for up to 1 month. To serve, remove the plastic wrap and defrost in the refrigerator overnight. Reheat in an oven preheated to 350°F (180°C) for 30–40 minutes until piping hot (cover with foil if it starts to brown). Alternatively, reheat portions in a microwave on medium for 2–3 minutes, or until piping hot. Let stand for 5 minutes before serving.

serves 6

**prep 15 mins,
plus cooling
• cook 1 hr**

**9in (23cm)
loose-bottomed
fluted tart pan
• baking beans**

Spicy beef pies

Aromatic, tender beef encased in crumbly pastry.

INGREDIENTS

2 tbsp olive oil

9oz (250g) round (rump) steak

1 onion, finely chopped

pinch of sea salt

2 garlic cloves, finely chopped

1–2 fresh green jalapeño chile peppers,
   seeded and finely chopped

2in (5cm) piece of fresh ginger,
   finely chopped

1 tsp coriander seeds, crushed

4$\frac{1}{2}$oz (125g) mushrooms, finely chopped

$\frac{1}{2}$ tsp cayenne pepper

all-purpose flour

1 sheet prepared dough for an
   8–9in (20–23cm) pie

1 egg, lightly beaten, for egg wash

METHOD

1 Preheat the oven to 400°F (200°C). Heat 1 tablespoon of the oil in a large frying pan over medium-high heat. Add the steak and cook, browning for about 3 minutes on each side to seal. Remove from the pan and set aside.

2 Heat the remaining oil over low heat. Add the onion and salt, and cook for about 5 minutes until soft. Add the garlic, chiles, ginger, and crushed coriander, and cook, stirring, for 2 minutes until fragrant. Add the mushrooms, season with the cayenne, and continue cooking over low heat for 5 minutes until the mushrooms soften and begin to release their juices.

3 Slice the reserved steak into strips, and return to the pan along with 1 tablespoon of water. Cook, stirring often, for about 2 minutes until the mixture is thick and moist, but not runny. Set aside to cool.

4 On a floured work surface, roll the pastry into a rectangle, and cut into four equal squares, 6–7in (15–18cm). Moisten each square around the edges with a little water. Divide the meat and onion filling into 4 equal portions, and spoon each one into the middle of a square. Bring together the opposite corners of each pastry square to form a triangle, pinching the edges together to seal. Brush all over with the egg wash, and bake in the oven for 20–30 minutes until golden. Serve hot.

FREEZING INSTRUCTIONS Let stand to cool completely, then wrap in wax paper and 2 layers of plastic wrap and freeze for up to 3 months. To serve, remove the plastic wrap and defrost in the refrigerator overnight. Reheat in a microwave on high for 2–3 minutes, turn, and heat for 2–3 minutes more, or until piping hot. Let stand for 5 minutes before serving.

serves 2

prep 20 mins
• cook 50 mins

Olive and anchovy open tart

Common pantry ingredients make this a perfect dish when time is short.

INGREDIENTS

1 x 17.3oz (425g) box frozen puff pastry sheets, thawed
1 egg, lightly beaten, for egg wash
$^1/_4$ cup tomato purée or tomato sauce
12 flat anchovy fillets, drained
12 pitted black olives
freshly ground black pepper

METHOD

1 Preheat the oven to 400°F (200°C). On a lightly floured work surface, place 1 sheet of puff pastry on top of the other. Roll out the pastry into a single sheet to a thickness of $^3/_8$in (4cm), and lay it on a baking sheet. Using a knife, score a line about 2in (5cm) in from the edge all the way around to form a border, but do not cut all the way through the pastry. Next, using the edge of the knife, score the pastry all the way around the outer edges.

2 Brush the border with the egg wash, then smooth the tomato sauce over the inside area, right up to the edges. Lay the anchovies and olives evenly over the tart so that everyone gets a taste of each, and season with pepper.

3 Bake for 15 minutes until the pastry is cooked and the edges are puffed and golden. Cut into 6 squares and serve warm.

FREEZING INSTRUCTIONS Let stand to cool completely, then wrap in wax paper and 2 layers of plastic wrap, and freeze for up to 1 month. To serve, remove the plastic wrap and defrost in the refrigerator overnight. Reheat portions in a microwave on medium for 3–4 minutes until piping hot. Let stand for 5 minutes before serving.

GOOD WITH A crisp green salad.

serves 6

prep 15 mins
• cook 15 mins

Chicken and sweet corn pie

Creamy and filling with a flaky pastry lid—this pie makes a generous lunch.

INGREDIENTS

2 tbsp olive oil

3 skinless, boneless chicken breast halves,
  cut into bite-sized chunks

sea salt and freshly ground black pepper

1 onion, finely chopped

1 tbsp all-purpose flour

²⁄₃ cup (150ml) heavy whipping cream

1¼ cups hot vegetable stock

1 x 12oz (350g) can whole kernel
  corn, drained

handful of flat-leaf parsley,
  finely chopped

half of a 17.3oz (425g) box frozen puff pastry
  sheets (1 sheet), thawed as package directs

1 large egg, lightly beaten, for egg wash

METHOD

1 Preheat the oven to 400°F (200°C). Heat 1 tablespoon of the oil in a large frying pan over medium-high heat. Season the chicken with salt and pepper. Add to the pan and cook, stirring, for 7–10 minutes until golden brown all over. Remove from the pan, and set aside.

2 Heat the remaining oil over low heat and add the onion and a pinch of salt. Cook gently for 5 minutes until soft. Remove from the heat and stir in the flour and a little cream. Return the pan to low heat and add the remaining cream and the stock, stirring for 5–8 minutes until the mixture thickens. Stir in the corn and parsley and season with salt and pepper.

3 Spoon the mixture into a 9in (23cm) pie pan. On a floured work surface, roll out the pastry so there is a border all around, extending about 2in (5cm) beyond the pie pan. Cut out a strip of pastry 1in (2.5cm) in from the edge to make a collar. Moisten the edge of the pie pan with water; fit the pastry strip all the way around, and press down firmly. Brush the collar with a little egg wash, then top with the pastry lid. Trim away the excess. Using your finger and thumb, pinch or press the edges together to seal.

4 Brush the top with the egg wash, cut a slit to let steam escape during cooking, and bake for 30–40 minutes until the pastry is golden and puffed. Serve hot.

FREEZING INSTRUCTIONS Let stand to cool completely, then wrap in plastic wrap and foil and freeze for up to 3 months. To serve, unwrap and defrost in the refrigerator overnight. Reheat in a microwave on high for 3–4 minutes, rotate the pan, and heat for 3–4 minutes more, or until piping hot. Let stand for 5 minutes before serving.

serves 4

prep 15 mins
• cook 1 hr

9in (23cm)
pie pan or
4 individual
pie pans

Lamb and pea pie

Fragrant spiced lamb with crumbly golden shortcrust topping.

INGREDIENTS

1–2 tbsp olive oil

1 onion, finely chopped

sea salt and freshly ground black pepper

2 garlic cloves, finely chopped

12oz (350g) lamb leg steaks, cut into
    bite-sized pieces

1 tsp ground turmeric

$\frac{1}{2}$ tsp ground allspice

2 tbsp all-purpose flour

4 cups hot vegetable stock

2 waxy all-purpose potatoes, peeled
    and cut into small cubes

1 cup frozen peas, thawed

1 sheet prepared dough for an
    8–9in (20–23cm) pie

1 egg, lightly beaten, for egg wash

METHOD

1 Heat 1 tablespoon of the oil in a large saucepan over low heat. Add the onion and a pinch of salt, and cook gently for about 5 minutes until soft. Increase the heat to medium, and add a little extra oil if needed. Add the lamb, and sprinkle with the turmeric and allspice. Cook, stirring occasionally, for 6–8 minutes until the lamb is browned all over.

2 Remove from the heat, and stir in the flour and 1 tablespoon of the stock. Return to the heat, and pour in the remaining stock. Bring to a boil, reduce the heat to low, and add the potatoes. Simmer gently, stirring occasionally so that they don't stick, for about 20 minutes until the potatoes have cooked and the sauce has thickened. Add the peas, and season well with salt and pepper.

3 Meanwhile, preheat the oven to 400°F (200°C). Spoon the meat filling into a 9in (23cm) pie pan. On a floured work surface, roll out the pastry so that it is about 2in (5cm) larger than the top of the pie pan. Cut out a strip of pastry about 1in (2.5cm) in from the edge to make a collar. Moisten the edge of the pie pan with a little water; fit the pastry strip all the way around, and press down firmly. Brush the pastry collar with a little of the egg wash, then top with the pastry lid. Trim away the excess pastry. Using your finger and thumb, pinch together the edges to seal.

4 Brush the top of the pie all over with the remaining egg wash. Using a sharp knife, make 2 slits in the top to allow steam to escape. Bake for 30–40 minutes until cooked and golden all over. Serve hot.

FREEZING INSTRUCTIONS Let stand to cool completely, then wrap in plastic wrap and foil and freeze for up to 3 months. To serve, unwrap and defrost in the refrigerator overnight. Reheat in a microwave on high for 3–4 minutes, rotate the pan, and heat for 3–4 minutes more, or until piping hot. Let stand for 5 minutes before serving.

serves 4

prep 15 mins
• cook 1 hr
15 mins

9in (23cm)
pie pan

Fish and leek pie

You can use any white fish for this pie—choose the freshest available.

INGREDIENTS

1 tbsp olive oil
1 onion, finely chopped
sea salt and freshly ground black pepper
4 leeks, thinly sliced
1 tbsp all-purpose flour
$^2/_3$ cup hard cider, apple cider,
    or unsweetened apple juice
handful of flat-leaf parsley, finely chopped

$^2/_3$ cup heavy whipping cream
1$^1/_2$lb (675g) raw skinless, boneless
    white fish, such as haddock or pollack,
    cut into chunks
half of a 17.3oz (425g) box frozen puff pastry
    sheets (1 sheet), thawed as package directs
1 egg, lightly beaten, for egg wash

METHOD

1 Preheat the oven to 400°F (200°C). Heat the oil in a large frying pan over low heat. Add the onion and a pinch of salt, and cook gently for about 5 minutes until soft. Add the leeks, and continue to cook gently for another 10 minutes until softened. Remove from the heat, stir in the flour, and add a little of the cider. Return to the heat, pour in the remaining cider, and cook for 5–8 minutes until thickened.

2 Stir in the parsley and cream and cook 1–2 minutes, then remove from the heat and stir in the fish. Spoon the mixture into a 9in (23cm) pie pan or other baking dish. Season well with salt and pepper.

3 Roll out the pastry on a floured work surface so that it is about 2in (5cm) larger all around than the top of the pie pan. Cut out a strip of pastry about 1in (2.5cm) in from the edge to make a collar. Moisten the edge of the pie pan with a little water, fit the pastry strip all the way around, and press down firmly. Brush the pastry collar with a little of the egg wash, then top with the pastry lid. Trim away the excess, and pinch together the edges to seal. Using a sharp knife, make 2 slits in the top to allow steam to escape.

4 Brush the top of the pie all over with the egg wash, and bake for 20–30 minutes until the pastry is puffed and golden. Serve hot.

FREEZING INSTRUCTIONS Let stand to cool completely, then wrap in plastic wrap and foil and freeze for up to 3 months. To serve, unwrap and defrost in the refrigerator overnight. Reheat in a microwave on high for 3–4 minutes, rotate the pan, and heat for 3–4 minutes more, or until piping hot. Let stand for 5 minutes before serving.

serves 4

prep 15 mins
• cook 50 mins

9in (23cm)
pie pan

Pea and pancetta tart

Frozen peas provide a wonderful sweetness to this salty tart.

INGREDIENTS

1 sheet prepared dough for an 8–9in (20–23cm) pie
all-purpose flour
2 large eggs, plus 1 extra yolk, lightly beaten, for egg wash
1 tbsp olive oil
1 onion, finely chopped
sea salt and freshly ground black pepper
4$\frac{1}{2}$oz (125g) pancetta, cut into cubes
6 fresh sage leaves, coarsely chopped
1$\frac{1}{2}$ cups frozen peas
$\frac{2}{3}$ cup heavy whipping cream

METHOD

1 Preheat the oven to 400°F (200°C). Roll out the pastry on a floured work surface, and use to line the tart pan with a removable bottom. Trim away the excess, line the pastry shell with parchment paper, and fill with baking beans. Bake for 15–20 minutes until the edges of the pastry are golden. Remove the beans and paper, brush the bottom of the shell with a little of the egg wash, and return to the oven for 2–3 minutes to crisp. Remove from the oven and set aside. Reduce the oven temperature to 350°F (180°C).

2 Meanwhile, heat the oil in a large frying pan over low heat. Add the onion and a pinch of salt, and cook gently for about 5 minutes until soft. Add the pancetta and sage, increase the heat a little, and cook for 6–8 minutes until the pancetta is golden and crispy. Stir in the peas, and season with salt and pepper.

3 Spoon the onion and pancetta mixture into the pastry shell, and level the top. Mix together the cream and the 2 eggs, and season well. Carefully pour the cream mixture over the filling to cover. Bake for 20–30 minutes until set and golden. Let cool for 10 minutes before removing the sides of the pan.

FREEZING INSTRUCTIONS Let stand to cool completely, then wrap in wax paper and 2 layers of plastic wrap, and freeze for up to 1 month. To serve, remove the plastic wrap and defrost in the refrigerator overnight. Reheat in an oven preheated to 350°F (180°C) for 30–40 minutes until piping hot (cover with foil if it starts to brown). Alternatively, reheat portions in a microwave on medium for 2–3 minutes, or until piping hot. Let stand for 5 minutes before serving.

GOOD WITH Tomato salad.

serves 4–6

prep 10 mins,
plus cooling
• cook 1 hr
15 mins

8in (20cm) round
loose-bottomed
straight-sided
tart pan
• baking beans

Cheese and onion pie

Tangy Cheddar cheese perfectly complements onion to make a mouth-watering pie.

INGREDIENTS
1 tbsp olive oil
1 large onion, finely chopped
sea salt and freshly ground black pepper
2 large eggs
1 cup shredded sharp Cheddar cheese
2 sheets prepared dough for an 8–9in (20–23cm) pie

METHOD
1 Preheat the oven to 400°F (200°C). Heat the oil in a saucepan over low heat. Add the onion and a pinch of salt, and cook for a couple of minutes until translucent and just starting to soften. Scrape into a bowl and leave to cool completely. Lightly beat 1 of the eggs, and stir into the cooled onion. Stir in the cheese and season with salt and pepper.

2 Roll out one piece of pastry on a floured work surface. Use it to line pan, folding over the edges, and fill with the cheese and onion mixture. Moisten the edge of the pastry with a little water, then top with the other circle of pastry. Trim away the excess, then pinch together with your finger and thumb to seal. Using a sharp knife, make two slits in the top of the pie to allow steam to escape.

3 Lightly beat the remaining egg to make an egg wash, and brush all over the top of the pie. Bake in the oven for 25–35 minutes until cooked and golden.

FREEZING INSTRUCTIONS Let stand to cool completely, then wrap in wax paper and 2 layers of plastic wrap and freeze for up to 3 months. To serve, remove the plastic wrap and defrost in the refrigerator overnight. Reheat portions in a microwave on medium for 2–3 minutes, turn, and heat for 2–3 minutes more, or until piping hot. Let stand for 5 minutes before serving.

GOOD WITH A mixed salad and boiled or steamed new potatoes.

serves 4

prep 15 mins,
plus cooling
• cook 40 mins

8in (20cm)
round pie pan

Mushroom and ricotta pies with red pepper pesto

To prevent damp pastry, leave the sides slightly open to allow steam to escape.

INGREDIENTS

$\frac{1}{2}$ cup olive oil

1 onion, sliced

sea salt and freshly ground black pepper

2 red bell peppers, sliced

2 garlic cloves, crushed

finely grated zest and juice of 1 lemon

10oz (300g) small mushrooms, halved

1 leek, white part only, thinly sliced

2 sheets pre-rolled puff pastry (preferably made with butter), thawed if frozen; or 1 x 17.3oz (425g) box frozen puff pastry sheets, thawed as package directs

7oz (200g) ricotta cheese

1 large egg yolk, lightly beaten

METHOD

1 Preheat the oven to 400°F (200°C), and line a baking sheet with parchment paper. To make the red pepper pesto, heat 3 tablespoons of the oil in a heavy frying pan over low heat. Add the onion and a pinch of salt, and cook gently for 5 minutes until soft. Add the peppers, and cook, stirring frequently, for 10–15 minutes until tender. Transfer the onion mixture to a food processor. Add the garlic and lemon zest and juice, and pulse, turning the machine on and off, until the mixture becomes a chunky purée. Season with salt and pepper. Set aside.

2 Heat another 3 tablespoons of the oil in a clean large heavy frying pan over medium heat. Add the mushrooms and the leek, and cook, stirring, for 5 minutes until the mushrooms have lightly browned. Set aside.

3 Cut each pastry sheet into 4 squares. Divide the ricotta equally among 4 of the squares, leaving a $\frac{1}{2}$in (1cm) border all around the edges. Spoon the mushroom and leek mixture evenly over the ricotta. Using a sharp knife, cut diagonal slashes across the surface of the remaining 4 pastry squares, being careful not to slice all the way through, then lay one evenly over the top of each square that has the ricotta-mushroom filling. Pinch and twist together the corners of the pies to seal, and brush the tops with the egg yolk to glaze.

4 Place the pies on the baking sheet, and bake for 25 minutes until golden brown. Serve with the red pepper pesto.

FREEZING INSTRUCTIONS Let stand to cool completely, then wrap in wax paper and a double layer of plastic wrap, and freeze for up to 1 month. To serve, remove the plastic wrap and defrost in the refrigerator overnight. Reheat in a microwave on medium for 3–4 minutes until piping hot. Let stand for 5 minutes before serving. The pesto can be kept in the refrigerator topped up with oil for up to 2 weeks.

GOOD WITH A leafy green salad.

serves 4

prep 25 mins • cook 45 mins

blender or food processor

Curried vegetable pies

These individual pies make a convenient and tasty snack.

INGREDIENTS

2 carrots, diced
2 all-purpose waxy potatoes, peeled and finely diced
2 sheets prepared dough for an 8–9in (20–23cm) pie
all-purpose flour
1 egg, lightly beaten, for egg wash
1 tbsp prepared curry paste or 1 tsp Madras curry powder
2 tbsp Greek-style plain yogurt
1 garlic clove, finely chopped
1in (2cm) fresh ginger, finely chopped
2 scallions, thinly sliced
handful of fresh cilantro, chopped
juice of $1/2$ lemon
salt and freshly ground black pepper

METHOD

1 Preheat the oven to 400°F (200°C). Boil the carrots and potatoes in a pan of salted water for about 15 minutes until soft. Drain well.

2 Roll out each sheet of pastry on a floured work surface, then use a 6in (15cm) plate or saucer as a template to cut out two circles from each sheet. Put the pastry rounds on a parchment-lined baking sheet, and brush the edges with a little of the egg wash.

3 Put the carrots and potatoes in a bowl, and gently mix together with the curry paste and yogurt. Add the garlic, ginger, scallions, cilantro, and lemon juice, and season well with salt and pepper. Stir through gently until well mixed.

4 Divide the vegetable mixture evenly among the pastry circles, spooning it into the center of each one. Fold over the pastry to make a half-moon shape, and pinch the edges together to seal. Using a sharp knife, make 2 slashes in the top of each pie, then brush all over with the remaining egg wash. Bake for 20–30 minutes until golden. Serve hot or cold.

FREEZING INSTRUCTIONS Let stand to cool completely, then wrap in wax paper and a double layer of plastic wrap, and freeze for up to 3 months. To serve, remove the plastic wrap and defrost in the refrigerator overnight. Reheat in a microwave on medium for 3–4 minutes, or until piping hot. Let stand for 5 minutes before serving.

GOOD WITH A crisp green salad.

serves 2

prep 15 mins
• cook 45 mins

6in (15cm)
saucer or plate

Gruyère, potato, and thyme tartlets

These individual tartlets are ideal for a light lunch.

INGREDIENTS

2 sheets prepared dough, each large enough
   for an 8–9in (20–23cm) pie
all-purpose flour
2 large eggs, plus 1 extra, lightly beaten, for egg wash
2 all-purpose waxy potatoes, peeled and cut into $\frac{1}{2}$in (1cm) cubes
2 tbsp olive oil
1 small onion, very finely diced
a few sprigs of fresh thyme, leaves picked
$\frac{2}{3}$ cup shredded Gruyère cheese
1 cup heavy whipping cream
sea salt and freshly ground black pepper

METHOD

1 Preheat the oven to 400°F (200°C). Roll out the pastry on a floured surface and use to line the 4 tart pans. Trim the excess, line the pastry shells with parchment paper, and fill with baking beans. Bake in the oven for 15–20 minutes until the edges are golden. Remove the beans and paper, brush the bottoms with egg wash, and return to the oven for 2–3 minutes to crisp. Remove, set aside, and reduce the oven temperature to 350°F (180°C).

2 Boil the potatoes in a small pan of salted water for about 5 minutes until just starting to soften but still not tender; do not overcook. Drain.

3 Meanwhile, heat the oil in a large nonstick frying pan over low heat. Add the onion and a pinch of salt, and cook gently for about 5 minutes until soft. Add the partially boiled potatoes and the thyme, and season with some pepper. Cook, stirring occasionally, for about 10 minutes until the potatoes begin to brown.

4 Remove from the heat, and stir in the Gruyère cheese. Taste, and season some more if needed. Divide the mixture evenly among the pastry shells. Mix together the cream and the 2 eggs, then carefully pour equal amounts into each tart. Place the tarts on a baking sheet, and bake in the oven for 20–30 minutes until set and golden. Serve hot.

FREEZING INSTRUCTIONS Let stand to cool completely, then wrap in wax paper and a double layer of plastic wrap, and freeze for up to 1 month. To serve, remove the plastic wrap and defrost in the refrigerator overnight. Reheat in a microwave on medium for 1–2 minutes, rotate the tarts, and heat for 1–2 minutes more, or until piping hot. Let stand for 5 minutes before serving.

serves 4

prep 20 mins
• cook 1 hr

4 tart pans,
4in (10cm)
• baking beans

Mixed mushroom and walnut tart

Exotic mushrooms will give this vegetarian tart a fuller flavor.

INGREDIENTS

1 sheet prepared dough for an 8–9in (20–23cm) pie
all-purpose flour
2 large eggs, plus 1 extra yolk, lightly beaten, for egg wash
3–4 tbsp olive oil
5oz (140g) fresh exotic or wild mushrooms
　(such as porcini or shiitake), coarsely chopped
7oz (200g) cultivated mushrooms, coarsely chopped
3 garlic cloves, finely chopped
1/2 cup walnut halves and pieces, coarsely chopped
sea salt and freshly ground black pepper
2 handfuls of fresh spinach leaves, coarsely chopped
1 cup heavy whipping cream

METHOD

1 Preheat the oven to 400°F (200°C). Roll out the pastry on a floured work surface, and use to line a tart pan with a removable bottom. Trim away the excess, line the pastry shell with parchment paper, and fill with baking beans. Bake for 15–20 minutes until the edges are golden. Remove the beans and paper, brush the bottom of the shell with a little of the egg wash, and return to the oven for 2–3 minutes to crisp. Remove from the oven and set aside. Reduce the oven temperature to 350°F (180°C).

2 Heat the oil in a large deep-sided frying pan over low heat. Add the mushrooms, garlic, and walnuts, and season well with salt and pepper. Cook, stirring occasionally, for about 10 minutes until the mushrooms release their juices. Add the spinach, and cook, stirring, for 5 minutes until just wilted. Spoon the mixture into the pastry shell.

3 Mix together the cream and the 2 eggs. Season well with salt and pepper. Carefully pour the cream mixture over the mushroom filling. Season with a pinch of pepper, and bake for 15–20 minutes until set. Let stand to cool for 10 minutes before removing the sides from the pan. Serve hot or cold.

FREEZING INSTRUCTIONS Let stand to cool completely, then wrap in wax paper and a double layer of plastic wrap, and freeze for up to 1 month. To serve, remove the plastic wrap and defrost in the refrigerator overnight. Reheat portions in a microwave on medium for 1–2 minutes, turn, then heat for 1–2 minutes more, or until piping hot. Let stand for 5 minutes before serving. Alternatively, reheat in an oven preheated to 350°F (180°C) for 30 minutes until piping hot (cover with foil if it starts to brown).

serves 6

prep 15 mins,
plus cooling
• cook 1 hr

5 x 14in
(12.5 x 35cm)
rectangular
loose-bottomed
fluted tart pan
• baking beans

Beef ragù

Easy and versatile, the ragù is meat-based sauce that can be paired with pasta, rice, or potatoes. This beef version will make an excellent staple for your freezer.

INGREDIENTS

4 tbsp olive oil
2 large onions, finely diced
1¹/₂lb (675g) lean beef, cut into ¹/₂in (1cm) cubes
8 garlic cloves, finely diced
1¹/₄ cups red wine
2 x 28oz (800g) cans chopped tomatoes
4 bay leaves
1 tsp fresh thyme leaves, finely chopped
sea salt and freshly ground black pepper

METHOD

1 Heat the oil in a large heavy-based saucepan, add the onions, and cook on a medium heat, stirring frequently, for 5 minutes or until soft. Add the beef and cook, stirring frequently, for another 5 minutes or until no longer pink. Add the garlic and cook for another minute, then pour in the wine and allow to simmer and reduce for 5 minutes.

2 Add the tomatoes, bay leaves, and thyme, bring to a boil, then reduce the heat and simmer for 30 minutes, stirring occasionally. Taste and season with salt and pepper. Serve hot.

FREEZING INSTRUCTIONS Let stand to cool completely, then remove and discard the bay leaves. Divide the ragù evenly among 4 sealable freezer bags (2 portions per bag) and freeze for up to 6 months. To serve, defrost in the refrigerator overnight, then reheat in a pan. Simmer gently for 15–20 minutes, adding hot water if needed, or until piping hot.

GOOD WITH Pasta or creamy mashed potatoes.

serves 8

prep 20 mins
• cook 45 mins

Lamb and eggplant ragù

Using lean lamb for this recipe will help the meat keep well in the freezer.

INGREDIENTS
$^1/_2$ cup olive oil
2 onions, finely diced
2 medium eggplants, cut into $^1/_2$in (1cm) cubes
1lb (450g) lean lamb, cut into $^1/_2$in (1cm) cubes
6 garlic cloves, finely chopped
3 x 14oz (400g) cans chopped tomatoes
3 bay leaves
1 tbsp dried oregano
handful of flat-leaf parsley, chopped
sea salt and freshly ground black pepper

METHOD
1 Heat the oil in a large heavy-based saucepan, add the onions, and cook over medium heat, stirring, for 3 minutes. Add the eggplants and cook, stirring frequently, for 5 minutes or until starting to brown. Add the lamb, combine well, and cook, stirring frequently, for 5 minutes or until no longer pink.

2 Stir in the garlic and cook for 1 minute. Add the tomatoes, bay leaves, oregano, and parsley, bring to a boil, then reduce the heat and simmer for 20 minutes, stirring occasionally. Taste and season with sea salt and freshly ground black pepper.

3 Let cool completely, then remove the bay leaves and discard. Divide the ragù evenly among 4 freezer bags, seal, and freeze for up to 3 months.

4 To serve, defrost overnight in the refrigerator, then transfer to a saucepan and heat until piping hot.

FREEZING INSTRUCTIONS Let stand to cool completely, then remove and discard the bay leaves. Divide the ragù evenly among 4 sealable freezer bags (2 portions per bag), ensuring the meat is well covered by the sauce, and freeze for up to 3 months. To serve, defrost in the refrigerator overnight, then reheat in a pan. Simmer gently for 15–20 minutes, adding hot water if needed, or until piping hot.

GOOD WITH Pasta or rice.

serves 8

prep 20 mins
• cook 35 mins

Ragù of venison with wild mushrooms

This slowly simmered stew concentrates all the rich flavors of venison and mushrooms.

INGREDIENTS

1 tbsp olive oil
1 tbsp butter
4 shallots, sliced
4oz (115g) sliced bacon, diced
1½lb (675g) venison, cut into 1½in (3.5cm) cubes
1 tbsp all-purpose flour
3 tbsp brandy
1¼ cups beef stock
9oz (250g) wild mushrooms, sliced
1 tbsp tomato paste
1 tbsp Worcestershire sauce
1 tsp dried oregano
salt and freshly ground black pepper

METHOD

1 Heat the oil and butter in a large flameproof casserole over medium-high heat. Add the shallots and bacon and cook, stirring often, until the shallots begin to brown.

2 Add the venison and cook, stirring, for about 4 minutes, or until evenly colored. Stir in the flour and cook for 2 minutes, until beginning to brown. Add the brandy and stir for 30 seconds, then add the stock and mushrooms. Bring to a boil, stirring. Stir in the tomato paste, Worcestershire sauce, and oregano, and season with salt and pepper.

3 Reduce the heat to low, cover, and simmer the ragù for 45 minutes–1½ hours, or until the venison is tender (the cooking time will depend on the cut of meat—loin takes less time than shoulder). Serve hot.

FREEZING INSTRUCTIONS Let stand to cool, then transfer to a sealable freezerproof container or freezer bags, making sure the meat is well covered by the sauce. Freeze for up to 3 months. To serve, defrost in the refrigerator overnight, then reheat in a pan. Simmer gently for 15–20 minutes, adding hot water or hot stock if needed, or until piping hot.

GOOD WITH Pasta, plain boiled rice, or potatoes.

serves 4

prep 15 mins
• cook 1–1¾ hrs

flameproof
casserole

Rich tomato sauce

Eaten on its own with pasta or used in other recipes, this sauce is so useful that it won't stay in the freezer for long!

INGREDIENTS
4 tbsp olive oil
4 garlic cloves, finely sliced
2 x 28oz (800g) cans whole tomatoes, chopped
2 tbsp tomato paste or purée
2 tsp dried oregano
2 bay leaves
sea salt and freshly ground black pepper
2 heaping tsp pesto

METHOD
1 Heat the oil in a large heavy-based saucepan, add the garlic, and cook over low heat for a few seconds. Add the tomatoes and tomato paste or purée, bring to a boil, then add the oregano and bay leaves and simmer for 25 minutes, stirring occasionally.

2 Season with salt and pepper, cook for 2 minutes, then stir in the pesto and remove from heat.

FREEZING INSTRUCTIONS Let stand to cool completely, then remove and discard the bay leaves. Divide the sauce evenly among 4 sealable freezer bags (2 portions per bag) and freeze for up to 6 months. To serve, defrost in the refrigerator overnight, then reheat in a pan. Simmer gently for 15–20 minutes, adding hot water if needed, or until piping hot.

GOOD WITH Pasta or use to make a lasagna or moussaka.

serves 8

prep 10 mins
• cook 30 mins

healthy option

Spinach sauce

This is a lovely alternative to a tomato-based sauce.

INGREDIENTS
4 tbsp olive oil
2 large onions, finely diced
4 garlic cloves, finely sliced
2 red chiles, seeded and finely chopped
1¼lb (550g) baby spinach leaves, rinsed and coarsely chopped
1¼ cups dry white wine
2 tbsp all-purpose flour
3 cups milk
sea salt and freshly ground black pepper

METHOD
1 Heat the oil in a large heavy-based pan, add the onions, and cook over medium heat, stirring frequently, for 5 minutes or until soft. Stir in the garlic and chiles and cook for 2 minutes. Add the spinach and cook for 3 minutes or until wilted.

2 Add the wine and allow to simmer for 5 minutes or until reduced by half. Add the flour and combine well. Pour in half the milk and stir well to combine. Add the rest of the milk a little at a time, stirring constantly, and cook for 5 minutes or until you have a creamy sauce. Season well with salt and pepper.

FREEZING INSTRUCTIONS Let stand to cool completely, then divide the sauce evenly among 4 sealable freezer bags (2 portions per bag) and freeze for up to 3 months. To serve, defrost in the refrigerator overnight, then transfer to a pan with a little milk. Heat through gently until hot (but do not overcook).

GOOD WITH Chicken, fish, or new potatoes, or stir in some grated Cheddar cheese and serve with pasta.

serves 8

prep 15 mins
• cook 20 mins

healthy option

Make ice cream

Ice cream can be easily made by hand, or with a machine for a finer texture. You can add puréed fruit, nuts, or other flavors to create your own variations.

By hand

1 Split two vanilla beans and scrape out the seeds, reserving them for later. Add the beans to a pot with 2 cups heavy cream, and bring to a boil. Add $\frac{1}{3}$ cup of sugar, and stir until dissolved.

2 In a bowl, whisk 4 egg yolks until well combined, then strain the warm cream mixture into the eggs, stirring all the time. Add the reserved vanilla seeds, and stir.

3 Pour the mixture into a metal loaf pan or plastic container. Let it cool completely.

4 Once cool, put into the freezer. When frozen, double wrap with plastic wrap and freeze for up to 3 months.

With an ice cream machine

1 Prepare a custard (see steps 1 and 2 opposite) then cool it in a bowl set in a large bowl of ice. Stir continuously to prevent a skin from forming.

2 Pour the custard mixture into an ice cream maker, and process until thick and smooth. Transfer to a freezerproof container, and freeze until firm.

Make granita

Combine sugar, fruit juice, and water (or red or white wine) to make a syrup that can be frozen to create a light and refreshing dessert.

1 Slowly bring the ingredients to a boil, reduce the heat, and simmer for 2–3 minutes, stirring. Cool, pour into a shallow baking pan, and freeze. When half-frozen, use a fork to break up the frozen chunks.

2 Break up the crystals once or twice more until evenly frozen. Remove from the freezer 5–10 minutes before serving, to thaw slightly. Scrape up the frozen granita and serve in pre-chilled glasses.

Vanilla ice cream

Nothing beats creamy homemade vanilla ice cream.

INGREDIENTS

1¼ cups whole milk
1 vanilla bean, split lengthwise
½ cup sugar
3 large egg yolks
1¼ cups heavy cream

METHOD

1 Bring the milk and vanilla bean to a simmer in a heavy-bottomed medium saucepan over medium-low heat. Cover and let stand 30 minutes. Remove the vanilla bean and, using the tip of a small knife, scrape the beans from the pod back into the milk. Rinse the vanilla bean and reserve for another use, if desired.

2 Whisk together the sugar and egg yolks in a large bowl until the mixture is thick and pale. Gradually whisk in the warm milk then pour into the saucepan. Cook over low heat, stirring constantly with a wooden spoon, until the mixture coats the spoon (an instant-read thermometer will read 185°F/85°C). Do not boil. Strain through a wire sieve into a bowl. Cool completely, stirring often. Cover and refrigerate at least 2 hours, until thoroughly chilled. Whisk the cream into the cooled custard.

3 Pour into the container of an ice cream machine. Freeze according to the manufacturer's instructions. Transfer to an airtight, freezerproof container and freeze for at least 2 hours.

4 Scoop the frozen ice cream into bowls and serve.

FREEZING INSTRUCTIONS Freeze for up to 3 months. Remove the ice cream from the freezer 20–30 minutes before scooping.

GOOD WITH Fresh berries, or biscotti crumbled into the base of the serving glass.

serves 4

prep 25 mins,
plus cooling
and freezing
• cook 12 mins

allow at least
2 hrs for
freezing

ice cream
machine
desirable

Strawberry semifreddo

This is Italian ice cream with a twist—texture and sweetness are added with crushed meringues.

INGREDIENTS

vegetable oil
8 strawberries, hulled, plus more whole strawberries to decorate
1 cup heavy cream
$^1/_2$ cup confectioner's sugar
4oz (115g) plain meringue cookies, coarsely crushed
3 tbsp raspberry-flavored liqueur

For the coulis

8oz (225g) strawberries, hulled
1–2 tsp fresh lemon juice, brandy, or balsamic vinegar
$^1/_3$ cup confectioner's sugar, as needed

METHOD

1 Lightly brush the springform pan with vegetable oil. Line the bottom with parchment paper.

2 Purée the strawberries in a blender or food processor. Whip the cream with the confectioner's sugar just until soft peaks form. Fold into the strawberry purée, then fold in the crushed meringues and liqueur. Spread the mixture evenly in the pan. Cover and freeze for at least 6 hours or overnight.

3 Meanwhile, make the strawberry coulis. Purée the strawberries, then strain through a fine wire sieve to remove the seeds. Stir in the lemon juice, brandy, or balsamic vinegar, then the sugar, adding more sugar if needed.

4 Just before serving, remove the sides of the springform. Invert onto a platter and peel off the paper. Cut into slices, dipping a sharp knife into hot water between slices. Transfer each slice to a plate. Spoon the coulis around each serving and garnish each with a whole strawberry. Serve chilled.

FREEZING INSTRUCTIONS Freeze the semifreddo for up to 3 months. Rather than freezing the coulis, make it on the day you wish to serve the semifreddo.

serves 6–8

prep 20 mins, plus freezing

freeze for at least 6 hrs, or overnight if possible

8in (20cm) loose-bottomed springform pan • blender or food processor

White chocolate chip ice cream

With white chocolate chips in a rich, dark chocolate ice cream, this is double-chocolate heaven.

INGREDIENTS

1¼ cups whole milk
1 vanilla bean, split lengthwise
5oz (140g) bittersweet chocolate, coarsely chopped
3 large egg yolks
½ cup sugar
1¼ cups heavy cream
1 cup white chocolate chips

METHOD

1 Bring the milk and vanilla bean to a simmer in a heavy-bottomed medium saucepan over medium-low heat. Add the chocolate, let stand for a few minutes, then stir until the chocolate is melted. Cover and let stand 15 minutes. Remove the vanilla bean and, using the tip of a small knife, scrape the seeds from the pod back into the milk. Rinse the vanilla bean and reserve for another use, if desired.

2 Whisk together the egg yolks and sugar in a large bowl until the mixture becomes thick and pale. Gradually whisk in the warm milk mixture, then pour into the saucepan. Cook over low heat, stirring constantly with a wooden spoon, until the mixture coats the spoon (an instant-read thermometer will read 185°F/85°C). Do not boil. Strain through a wire sieve into a bowl. Cool completely, stirring often. Cover and refrigerate at least 2 hours, until thoroughly chilled. Stir the cream into the chilled custard.

3 Pour into the container of an ice cream machine. Freeze according to the manufacturer's instructions. Stir in the white chocolate chips. Transfer into an airtight freezerproof container and freeze for at least 2 hours. Scoop into bowls and serve.

FREEZING INSTRUCTIONS Freeze for up to 3 months. Remove the ice cream from the freezer 10–15 minutes before scooping.

serves 4

prep 25 mins,
plus cooling
and freezing
• cook 12 mins

allow at
least 2 hrs
for freezing

ice cream
machine
desirable

Pistachio ice cream

Pistachio is rightfully one of the most popular ice cream flavors.

INGREDIENTS
1¼ cups whole milk
3 large egg yolks
½ cup sugar
½ tsp pistachio or almond extract
few drops of green food coloring (optional)
1½ cups coarsely chopped pistachios, plus more for garnish
1¼ cups heavy cream, lightly whipped

METHOD

1 Bring the milk to a simmer in a heavy-bottomed saucepan over low heat. Beat the egg yolks and sugar in a large bowl until thick and pale. Whisk in the hot milk and then return to the saucepan. Cook the mixture over low heat, stirring constantly, until the custard thickens slightly and coats the back of a spoon. (An instant-read thermometer will read 185°F/85°C.) Do not boil.

2 Strain through a wire sieve back into the bowl and stir in the extract and a few drops of green food coloring, if using. Add the pistachios and let cool. Lightly whip the cream and fold into pistachio custard.

3 To freeze the ice cream by hand, pour the mixture into a freezerproof container and freeze for at least 3–4 hours, until icy. Whisk well. Freeze for 2 hours more and whisk again. Cover and freeze until ready to use. To freeze ice cream in an ice cream machine, pour the mixture into the freezing compartment and churn according to the manufacturer's instructions. Transfer to a freezerproof container, cover, and freeze until ready to use.

4 Scoop the ice cream into dessert glasses, sprinkle with chopped pistachios, and serve immediately.

FREEZING INSTRUCTIONS Freeze for up to 3 months. Remove the ice cream from the freezer 15 minutes before serving. Serve scoops scattered with chopped pistachios.

serves 4

prep 25–30 mins,
plus cooling
and freezing
• cook
12–15 mins

allow at least
6 hrs for freezing

ice cream
machine
desirable

Orange sorbet

Brightly colored and vibrantly flavored, a citrus sorbet is a satisfying summer dessert.

INGREDIENTS

2 large oranges
$^3/_4$ cup sugar
1 tbsp orange blossom water
1 large egg white

METHOD

1 Using a vegetable peeler, remove the zest from the oranges. Bring the sugar and $1^1/_4$ cups water to a simmer in a small saucepan over medium heat, stirring to dissolve the sugar. Add the orange zest and simmer over low heat for 10 minutes. Let cool slightly. Squeeze the juice from the oranges and stir into the syrup, along with the orange blossom water.

2 Strain the orange mixture into a bowl. Beat the egg white until soft peaks form. Gradually stir the orange mixture into the white.

3 To freeze the sorbet without an ice cream machine, pour the mixture into a metal baking dish. Freeze for at least 4 hours, until almost frozen solid. Mash with a fork to break up any ice crystals, then freeze until solid. If using an ice cream machine, follow the manufacturer's directions. Transfer to an airtight container and freeze until ready to use.

FREEZING INSTRUCTIONS Freeze for up to 3 months. Remove the sorbet from the freezer 15–30 minutes before serving to allow it to soften slightly.

serves 4

**prep 10 mins,
plus freezing
• cook 15 mins**

**allow at least
4 hrs for freezing**

**ice cream
machine
desirable**

Zesty lemon granita

Refreshing and not too sweet, this is a delicious dessert after a rich main course, or a cooling treat on a hot day.

INGREDIENTS
6 large lemons
$^2/_3$ cup sugar
twists of lemon peel, to decorate

METHOD
1 Using a vegetable peeler, remove the zest from 4 of the lemons in strips. Scrape away any white pith.

2 Bring the sugar and 1 cup water to a boil in a small saucepan over medium heat, stirring until the sugar dissolves. Increase the heat to high and boil for 5 minutes.

3 Pour the syrup into a shallow, freezerproof nonmetallic bowl. Stir in the lemon zest strips and let cool completely.

4 Meanwhile, grate the zest from the remaining 2 lemons. Squeeze the juice from all of the lemons and strain. You should have 1 cup of lemon juice. Remove and discard the lemon zest strips from the syrup. Stir in the lemon juice and grated lemon zest.

5 Transfer the dish to the freezer. Every 30 minutes or so, use a fork to stir and break up the frozen chunks. Continue to do this for about 4 hours or until the mixture has the texture of shaved ice. During the last 30 minutes or so, freeze serving dishes for the granita. Scoop the granita into the frozen dishes and serve immediately.

FREEZING INSTRUCTIONS Freeze for up to 1 month.

GOOD WITH A small sweet cookie.

serves 4

prep 5–10 mins, plus cooling and freezing • cook 5 mins

allow at least 4 hrs for freezing

shallow, freezerproof nonmetallic bowl

Espresso granita

The texture of granitas should be finely granular, like snow.

INGREDIENTS

$^1/_2$ cup sugar
$1^1/_4$ cups very strong espresso or French roast coffee, chilled
$^1/_2$ tsp pure vanilla extract

METHOD

1 Dissolve the sugar in $1^1/_4$ cups water in a small saucepan, stirring over medium heat until it boils. Increase the heat to high and boil, without stirring, for 5 minutes, to make a light syrup.

2 Pour the syrup into a shallow, freezerproof dish. Stir in the coffee and vanilla and let it cool completely.

3 Transfer to the freezer. Every 30 minutes or so, use a fork to break up the frozen chunks. Continue to do this for about 4 hours or until the mixture has the texture of shaved ice. During the last 30 minutes or so, place the serving dishes for the granita in the freezer. Scoop the granita into the dishes and serve immediately.

FREEZING INSTRUCTIONS Freeze for up to 1 month.

serves 4

prep 5 mins,
plus cooling
and freezing
• cook 5 mins

allow at least
4 hrs for
freezing

Page numbers in *italics* indicate illustrations.

DORLING KINDERSLEY WOULD LIKE TO THANK THE FOLLOWING:

Photographers
Steve Baxter, Martin Brigdale, Tony Cambio, Nigel Gibson, Francesco Guillamet, Adrian Heapy, Jeff Kauck, David Munns, David Murray, Ian O'Leary, Roddy Paine, William Reavell, Gavin Sawyer, William Shaw, Carole Tuff, Kieran Watson, Stuart West, Jon Whitaker

Recipe consultants
Peggy Fallon, Heather Whinney

Indexer
Susan Bosanko

Useful information

FREE PUBLIC LIBRARY UNION, NEW JERSEY

3 9549 00465 5529

Refrigerator and freezer storage guidelines

FOOD	REFRIGERATOR	FREEZER
Raw poultry, fish, and meat (small pieces)	2–3 days	3 months
Raw ground beef and poultry	1–3 days	3 months
Cooked whole roasts or whole poultry	2–3 days	9 months
Cooked poultry pieces	2–3 days	3 months
Soups and stocks	2–3 days	3–6 months
Stews	2–3 days	3 months
Pies	2–3 days	3–6 months

Oven temperature equivalents

FAHRENHEIT	CELSIUS	DESCRIPTION
225°F	110°C	Cool
250°F	130°C	Cool
275°F	140°C	Very low
300°F	150°C	Very low
325°F	160°C	Low
350°F	180°C	Moderate
375°F	190°C	Moderately hot
400°F	200°C	Hot
425°F	220°C	Hot
450°F	230°C	Very hot
475°F	240°C	Very hot